THE KIDS' WORLD ALMANAC® OF Animals and Pets

THE KIDS' WORLD ALMANAC® OF Animals and Pets

DEBORAH G. FELDER

Illustrated by John Lane

Interior and cover design: Nancy Eato

Published by The Trumpet Club
a division of Bantam Doubleday Dell Publishing Group, Inc.
666 Fifth Avenue, New York, New York 10103

Copyright © 1989 by Deborah G. Felder

All rights reserved. No part of this book may be reproduced or transmitted in any form or by any means, electronic or mechanical, including photocopying, recording or by any information storage and retrieval system, without the written permission of the Publisher, except where permitted by law. For information address: Pharos Books, New York, New York.

ISBN: 0-440-84161-5

Reprinted by arrangement with Pharos Books
Printed in the United States of America
January 1990

10 9 8 7 6 5 4 3 2 1
CW

To my husband, Daniel Burt,
and, of course, to Sly,
the Wonder Cat.

Contents

ACKNOWLEDGEMENTS

Many thanks to my friends and family for their enthusiasm, encouragement and support during the research and writing of this book. My very special thanks to the ASPCA, the editors of *Cat* and *Dog Fancy* magazines, Dr. Ellen Dierenfeld who is the New York Zoological Society animal nutritionist at the Bronx Zoo, June Foley, David Hendin, Mark Hoffman, Hana Lane, John Lane, Lisa Novak, Terri Revelle, Jay Sheppard of the U.S. Department of Interior, Fish and Wildlife Service, Robin Langley Sommer, and the UN Missions, Consulates General, Tourist Boards, and Cultural Institutes representing countries around the world.

Animals Around the World

This chapter features a *pride* of fascinating facts on mammals in the wild. You'll discover where they live, what they eat, how long they live, and how fast they run. You'll meet some animal celebrities and champions, find out about pets around the world, wild pets, state animals, extinct and endangered species, and more.

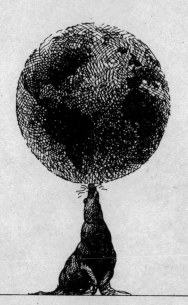

Mammals

In order to be classified as a mammal, an animal must have the following features:

• It has to be a vertebrate. Vertebrates are animals with a backbone. Invertebrates are animals without a backbone, such as worms, jellyfish, and insects.

• It has to have a four-chambered heart and be warm-blooded, which means its body temperature is kept fairly steady, regulated by insulating body coverings of fur, hair, or blubber. Cold-blooded animals like fish and reptiles cannot regulate their own body temperature—it depends upon that of their environment.

• It has to give birth to live young, which can be nourished with milk from the mother's mammary glands. The platypus and the spiny anteater are two mammals that lay eggs. However, the young of both these mammals are nourished by their mothers' milk.

Animals in the Wild

VITAL STATISTICS

Animal	Where Found	Habitat	Diet
Aardvark	Africa	Forests, plains; lives in dens	Ants, termites
Anteater	Central, South America	Tropical forests, savannas (grasslands)	Ants, termites
Antelope	Africa, Asian steppes	Savannas, forests; some in deserts, swamplands, mountains	Twigs, leaves, grasses
Armadillo	U.S., Central, South America	Tropical, sub-tropical regions, forests, open areas; lives in burrows	Termites, carrion (flesh of dead animals), vegetation
Baboon	Africa, Arabia	Savannas, rocky ground; tree-dwellers	Plants, small mammals, birds, birds' eggs
Badger	Western North America, Southeast Asia	Open, dry country, wooded regions, grasslands, forests, lowlands, mountainous regions; lives underground	Small animals, especially rodents; plants
Bat	Worldwide, except for Antarctica and the Arctic	Caves, crevices, burrows, buildings, trees, rocks	Insects, scorpions, spiders, small animals, blood of animals (vampire bats)

ANIMALS AROUND THE WORLD

Animal	Where Found	Habitat	Diet
Bear			
Black	North America, Asia	Forests	Mammals, fish, pine cones, berries, roots
Grizzly	North America	Mountainous forests	Deer, elk, moose, fish, berries
Polar	Arctic regions	Drifting ice floes, inland regions	Seals, fish, seaweed, grass, birds, caribou
Boar (wild pig)	Asia, Europe, North Africa, U.S.	Under rocks and fallen trees	Roots, fallen nuts, fruit, carrion, insect larvae
Bobcat	North America	Forests, deserts; makes lairs of dry moss or leaves in hollow logs, rock crevices, or thickets	Carnivorous— hunts and eats other animals
Buffalo	Africa Asia (India)	Forests, grasslands	Grasses
Bushbaby (monkey)	Africa	Forests	Fruits, plants, insects, small birds
Camel	Africa, Asia, Australia, Middle East	Deserts, Australian Outback	Thorny plants, dried grasses

Animal	Where Found	Habitat	Diet
Caribou	North America, Arctic region of Canada, Greenland	Forests, tundra	Lichen, grasses, mushrooms, twigs, weeds, berries
Cheetah	Africa, Near East	Open plains	Carnivorous—hunts and eats other animals
Chimpan-zee (ape)	Africa	Dense tropical forests and woodlands; tree-dwellers	Fruits, insects, vegetable matter
Civet (cat)	Africa, Asia, Southern Europe	Tree hollows, among rocks, some live partially in water	Small animals, fruit, vegetable matter
Coyote	North America, Central America	Prairies, deserts, open woodlands, brush country	Omnivorous—hunts and eats animals; also eats fruit
Deer	Africa, Europe; North, South America; Hawaii; Australia, New Zealand	Deserts, tundra, swamps, high mountainsides, forestlands	Grass, twigs, bark, shoots, buds
Dingo (wild dog)	Australia	Outback, countryside	Small animals, livestock

ANIMALS AROUND THE WORLD

Animal	Where Found	Habitat	Diet
Elephant	Africa, Asia	Thick jungles, savannas	Grasses and other vegetation, leaves, fruit, green nuts, a lot of water (20 to 40 gals. a day)
Elk	North America	Tundra, woodlands	Grasses, leaves, sometimes crops, haystacks, tree bark
Fox	Asia, Europe, Africa, U.S., Canada	Woodlands, farmlands; lives in dens	Mice, rabbits, birds, eggs, fruit
Giraffe	Africa	Savannas, open bush country	Chiefly acacia and mimosa leaves; twigs
Gnu (also called Wildebeest)	Africa	Savannas grasses	Twigs, leaves,
Gorilla (ape)	Africa	Tropical forests (rain or bamboo forests)	Leaves, stalks, bamboo shoots
Hare (rabbit)	Worldwide, except for Antarctic and Arctic regions	Grasslands, brush, desert and mountainous regions, open suburban areas. Shelter aboveground in grassy hollows called *forms*	Plants: grasses, tree bark, shrubs, grain, vegetables

Animal	Where Found	Habitat	Diet
Hedgehog	Africa, Asia, Britain, New Zealand	Fields, some in deserts; live in burrows	Animals, plants
Hippopotamus	Africa	Rivers, swamps	Feeds at night on water plants and shore vegetation, sometimes crops
Hyena	Africa, Asia	Caves, burrows	Carrion; also attacks small or helpless animals
Jackal	Africa, Europe, Southeast Asia	Open country; concealed by day in brush or thickets	Hunts small and large animals at dusk; also eats carrion, vegetable matter
Jaguar	Central, South America, U.S.	Swamps, jungles, other wooded regions; largest population of jaguars is in Amazon rain forests	Deer, tapirs, crocodiles, birds fish, sometimes cattle, horses, dogs
Kangaroo	Australia, Tasmania	Open forests, grasslands,	Plants
Kinkajou	Central, South America	Forests; tree-dwellers and mammals	Fruit, honey, insects, small birds
Koala	East coast of Australia	Forests; tree-dwellers	Eucalyptus leaves

ANIMALS AROUND THE WORLD

Animal	Where Found	Habitat	Diet
Lemur (monkey)	Madagascar, the Comoros	Wooded areas	Leaves, fruit, insects, eggs, small animals
Leopard	Africa, Asia	Bush country, semideserts, rain forests, mountains	Hunts and eats animals
Lion	Africa, India	Savannas	Hunts and eats animals; much hunting done by lionesses; lions can eat as much as 75 lbs. of meat at a single meal
Llama	South America	Semideserts; mountainous regions	Grass and other plants
Lynx	Asia, Europe, northern North America	Forests	Small mammals, birds, deer
Mongoose	Africa, Asia, Europe, Hawaii, West Indies	Variety; lives in rock crevices, holes, burrows	Small mammals, birds, reptiles, eggs, fruit
Monkey	Africa, Asia, Central, South America	Tropical forests; tree-dwellers ers, fruit, small	Leaves, birds, birds' eggs, flow- animals

THE KIDS' WORLD ALMANAC OF ANIMALS AND PETS

Animal	Where Found	Habitat	Diet
Moose	Northern North America, Europe, Asia	Forests, near lakes and streams bark	Water plants, grasses, herbs,
Ocelot (cat)	Texas, Mexico, Central, South America	Forests, brush country reptiles, birds	Small, medium-sized mammals,
Opossum	North, Central, South America	Lives in trees	Small animals, plants, insects, fruit
Orang-utan (ape)	Asia	Dense swamp forests; tree-dwellers	Fruit
Otter	Africa, Asia, Europe; North, Central, South America	Rain forests, near streams, rivers, lakes	Small mammals, fish
Panda	Asia (Nepal, China)	Mountains, mountain bamboo forests	Bamboo shoots, leaves, fruit, roots, flowers (Giant Panda eats mainly bamboo)
Puma (also known as mountain lion, cougar, and cata-mount)	North, South America to keep deer population down)	Mountains, jungles, deserts prefer deer (helps	Hunts and eats other animals;

Animal	Where Found	Habitat	Diet
Raccoon	North, South America	Woods, near water, suburban areas; lives in dens in hollow trees, drainage tiles, abandoned buildings, underground	Corn, nuts, fruit, berries, rodents, frogs
Reindeer	Northern North America, Europe, Asia, Arctic regions	Tundra, woodlands lichen (in winter)	Willow and birch shoots, grasses,
Rhino-ceros	Africa, Southeast Asia lands	Savannas, scrub forests, marsh-	Plants, grasses, fruit
Sable	Russia, Finland	Mountains	Small animals, birds, eggs
Shrew	Asia, Europe; North, Central, South America	Lives under vegetation, in burrows	Insects, plants, carrion; has a huge appetite
Skunk	North, South America	Open, wooded, desert regions; lives in dens	Eggs, birds, plants, worms, small mammals
Sloth	Tropical America	Forests; tree-dwellers, seldom descend to the ground	Tree leaves, twigs, fruit

Animal	Where Found	Habitat	Diet
Tiger	Eastern Russia, Asia, Southeast Asia	Grassy, swampy areas, forests; likes shady spots	Hunts and eats animals; needs to drink a good amount of water
Warthog	Africa	Lighly forested areas	Grass and other plants
Weasel	North, South America, Europe, Asia	Lives in dens made in holes in the ground, rock piles, hollow stumps	Rodents, fish, birds' eggs, frogs
Wolf	Asia, North America	Open and wooded areas	Mice, rabbits, birds, deer, moose, caribou
Wolverine	Northern North America, Europe, Asia	Mountainous, timbered areas, tundra	Frogs, larger animals like caribou, carrion; sometimes robs bears of their kills and raids cabins for food
Wombat	Australia	Grassy nests at the ends of burrows	Grasses, tree bark, shrubs
Yak	Asia (northern Tibet)	Plateaus at 14,000 to 20,000 ft. above sea level	Grass; said to eat snow in winter; needs a lot of water
Zebra	Africa	Grasslands, lightly wooded areas, dry upland plains	Grasses

A Bevy of Animal Facts

• **Dingoes,** wild dogs of Australia, howl, but do not bark like other dogs.

• **Jaguars** are afraid of dogs, even little ones. But, unlike most cats, jaguars like water. They can spend hours swimming in forest pools and rivers.

• **Elephant** tusks are extremely heavy and can weigh up to 300 pounds.

• An African antelope, the **sitatunga,** can sleep in the water of its marshland habitat.

• The duck-bill **platypus,** an Australian mammal, can eat its own weight in worms every day. An adult male platypus weighs about four pounds.

• **Elephants** are emotional animals. They "cry" when they feel frustrated. Elephants can also be loyal and loving to humans. They'll rescue humans from other elephants or from natural disasters and accidents.

• When a herd of **musk-oxen** is attacked by its worst enemies, arctic wolves and dogs, it forms a defensive circle with the young inside and the horned adults facing outward.

• Adult **otters** are very playful. They love to slide down steep mud- or snowbanks and plunge into water or snowdrifts.

• Adult **raccoons** can be savage fighters. They can hold off most dogs that attack them. In water, raccoons can drown their enemies.

• **Shrews** can die from the shock of a loud noise or a rough touch. A species of shrew, the two-armored, has a mesh of interlocking spines in its back. This network of spines is so strong it can support the weight of a person.

• Young **hippos** have babysitters. They are left in the care of a group of females and other young when their mothers go off to feed.

• **Aardvark,** in Afrikaans, the language of South Africa, means "Earth Pig."

• **Bears** retire to caves and sleep for long periods in the winter, but they don't undergo a true hibernation (staying inactive and asleep the entire winter). They will come out of their caves on warm days.

• **Bactrian camels** (two-humped) and **Dromedaries** (one-humped) store fat in their humps, not water, as is generally believed. But camels can fast and go without water for several days.

• The **cheetah** is sometimes called the hunting leopard. It can be tamed and was once used by people in India for hunting game.

• **Coyotes** sometimes breed with dogs to produce a species of canines called Coydogs.

• **Giraffes** are sometimes thought to be voiceless, because their voices are rarely heard. But giraffes actually make low calling sounds and moans.

• A **leopard** often stores the remains of its kill in the branches of a tree to prevent other animals from stealing it.

• The well-known **lion's** roar is usually heard in the evening before a night's hunting and again at dawn.

Animal Names

Animal	Male	Female
Ass	Jack	Jenny
Bear	Boar	Sow
Cattle	Bull	Cow
Chicken	Rooster	Hen
Deer	Buck	Doe
Duck	Drake	Duck
Elephant	Bull	Cow
Fox	Dog	Vixen
Goose	Gander	Goose
Horse	Stallion	Mare
Lion	Lion	Lioness
Pig	Boar	Sow
Rabbit	Buck	Doe
Sheep	Ram	Ewe
Tiger	Tiger	Tigress
Whale	Bull	Cow
Wolf	Dog	Bitch

Animal Collectives

A COLLECTIVE IS A GROUP OF ANIMALS OR PEOPLE. BELOW ARE SPECIAL WORDS THAT ARE USED TO DESCRIBE GROUPS OF ANIMALS.

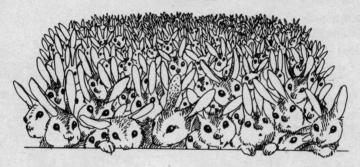

Ants—Colony

Badgers—Cete

Bears—Sleuth

Bees—Swarm, Grist

Birds—Flock, Flight, Volery

Boars—Sounder

Cattle—Herd, Drove

Cats—Clowder, Clutter

Chicks—Brood, Clutch

Clams—Bed

Crows—Murder

Ducks—Brace, Team

Elephants—Herd

Elk—Herd, Gang

Fish—School, Shoal

Foxes—Leash, Skulk

Geese—Flock, Gaggle

Gnats—Cloud, Hoard

Goats—Flock, Herd, Tribe, Trip

Gorillas—Band

Hares—Down, Hush

Hawks—Cast

Horses—Herd, Pair, Team

Kangaroos—Mob, Troop

Leopards—Leap

Lions—Pride

Monkeys—Troop

Oxen—Yoke

Peacocks—Muster

Pigs—Litter

Quail—Bevy, Covey

Rhinoceroses—Crash

Seals—Pod

Sheep—Flock, Drove

Swans—Bevy

Toads—Knot

Whales—Pod, Gang

Wolves—Pack

Animal Babies and Young

Antelope—Calf
Bear—Cub
Beaver—Kit
Bird—Fledgling, Nestling
Cat—Kitten, Kit
Cattle—Calf, Yearling
Codfish—Codling, Sprag
Deer—Fawn, Yearling
Dog—Pup, Puppy, Whelp
Duck—Duckling
Eagle—Eaglet
Eel—Elver
Elephant—Calf
Fish—Fingerling, Fry
Fox—Cub, Kit, Pup
Frog—Polliwog, Tadpole
Goat—Kid
Goose—Gosling
Hare—Leveret
Hen—Chick, Pullet
Hippopotamus—Calf
Horse—Filly (female),
    Colt (male), Foal, Yearling
Human—Infant, Newborn,
    Baby, Toddler, Child
Kangaroo—Joey
Lion—Cub
Owl—Owlet
Pig—Piglet, Shoat, Farrow,
    Suckling
Pigeon—Squab, Squeaker
Quail—Cheeper

Rabbit—Bunny, Kit
Rooster—Cockerel
Seal—Pup
Sea Lion—Pup
Shark—Cub
Sheep—Lamb, Lambkin,
    Cosset, Hog, Yearling
Swan—Cygnet
Tiger—Cub, Whelp
Turkey—Poult
Whale—Calf
Zebra—Foal

Eight Animals That Have Pouches

THESE ANIMAL MOTHERS ARE MARSUPIALS. THEY NURSE AND
CARRY THEIR BABIES IN ABDOMINAL POUCHES.

Bandicoot
Kangaroo
Koala
Marsupial Anteater

Opossum
Tasmanian Devil
Wallaby
Wombat

Some Different Names for Bears

BLACK BEAR   American Bear
Cinnamon Bear
Brown Bear
Himalayan Bear
Tibetan Bear
Moon Bear

GRIZZLY BEAR   Silvertip

POLAR BEAR   White Bear
Water Bear
Sea Bear
Ice Bear

Extinct and Endangered Species

Animals have been on earth for millions of years. In the time since the first animal appeared, thousands of species have become extinct (no longer in existence) through a natural process of evolution. But over the last few hundred years, many species have died out or become threatened because of humans. Hunting, pollution of the environment, and the destruction of animals' natural living space for human use have contributed to animal extinction and endangerment.

In 1973 the U.S. government passed a law called the Endangered Species Act. This law protects animals that are endangered and makes it possible for people to help them survive. It's important for humans to save animals around the world from extinction. All forms of life—and that includes animals *and* plants—are interdependent. Losing even a few life forms can be very harmful to humans.

Listed below are some extinct and endangered species.

MAMMALS
Cougar, Wisconsin
Elk, Eastern
Fox, Southern California
Sea Cow, Stellar's
Whale, Atlantic Great

BIRDS
Dodo
Hen, Heath
Parakeet, Carolina
Pigeon, Passenger
Thrush, Oahu

REPTILES AND AMPHIBIANS
Frog, Vegas Valley Leopard
Snake, St. Croix Ground

FISH
Dane, Grass Valley Speckled
Pupfish, Tecopa
Sucker, Harelip
Topminnow, Whiteline
Troup, Agassiz

ENDANGERED ANIMALS

MAMMALS

Bat, Ozark, Big-Eared
Bear, Grizzly or Brown
Bobcat
Camel, Bactrian
Cheetah
Chimpanzee
Cougar, Eastern
Elephant, Asian
Fox, San Joaquin Kit
Gorilla
Leopard
Lion, Asiatic
Monkey, Howler
Ocelot
Orangutan
Otter, Southern Sea
Panda, Giant
Panther, Florida
Prairie Dog, Utah
Rhinoceros, Black
Seal, Guadalupe Fur
Squirrel, Carolina Northern
  Flying and Mt. Graham Red
Tapir, Malayan
Tiger
Whale, Gray and Humpback
Wolf, Red
Yak, Wild
Zebra, Mountain

BIRDS

Condor, California
Crane, Wooded and
  Whooping
Curlew, Eskimo
Eagle, Bald
Falcon, Peregrine
Hawk, Hawaiian
Jay, Florida Scrub
Ostrich, West African
Parakeet, Golden
Parrot, Australian
Pelican, Brown
Tern, Roseate
Towhee, Inyo Brown
Vireo, Black-Capped
Woodpecker, Ivory-billed

REPTILES AND AMPHIBIANS

Alligator, American
Crocodile, American and Nile
Salamander, Desert Slender
Snake, Atlantic Salt Marsh
Toad, Puerto Rican
Tortoise, Gopher
Turtle, Alabama Red-Bellied
  and Plymouth Red-Bellied

FISH

Catfish, Yaqui
Chub, Bonytail
Trout, Gila

ENDANGERED ANIMALS THAT ARE GETTING A SECOND CHANCE

Environmentalists, conservationists, and animal activists the world over are working to restore wild animal populations. Here are some endangered wild animals that are being saved and protected.

• **Red Wolf** — Reestablished in the wild in coastal North Carolina. In 1988 two wolf pups were sighted.

• **Chesapeake Bay Bald Eagle** — Population has grown from 136 to 161. Bald eagles are also nesting once again at the site of the Quabbin Reservoir in Massachusetts.

• **Black-footed Ferret** — Successful breeding in captivity.

• **California Sea Otter** — A second population established off the coast of California near Los Angeles.

• **California Condor** — Rebuilding the population through breeding the last wild condors in captivity.

• **African wildlife** — Giraffes, gnus, zebras, and other endangered herd animals are protected on preserves in Africa. Those which breed successfully in captivity on such preserves, like the zebra, may rebuild their populations to the point where the animals can be reintroduced into the wild.

State Animals

ALABAMA
Bird: Yellowhammer

ALASKA
Bird: Willow Ptarmigan
Fish: King Salmon

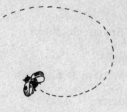

ARIZONA
Bird: Cactus Wren

ARKANSAS
Bird: Mockingbird
Insect: Honeybee

CALIFORNIA
Bird: California Valley Quail
Fish: California Golden Trout
Mammal: California Grizzly
Bear

COLORADO
Bird: Lark Bunting
Mammal: Rocky Mountain
Bighorn Sheep

CONNECTICUT
Bird: American Robin
Insect: Praying Mantis
Mammal: Sperm Whale

DELAWARE
Bird: Blue Hen Chicken
Insect: Ladybug

FLORIDA
Bird: Mockingbird

GEORGIA
Bird: Brown Thrasher

HAWAII
Bird: Nene (Hawaiian goose)

IDAHO
Bird: Mountain Bluebird
Horse: Appaloosa

ILLINOIS
Bird: Cardinal
Insect: Monarch Butterfly

INDIANA
Bird: Cardinal

IOWA
Bird: Eastern Goldfinch

KANSAS
Bird: Western Meadowlark

KENTUCKY
Bird: Kentucky Cardinal

LOUISIANA
Bird: Pelican

MAINE
Bird: Chickadee
Fish: Landlocked Salmon

MARYLAND
Bird: Baltimore Oriole
Fish: Rockfish
Insect: Baltimore Checkerspot
  Butterfly
Dog: Chesapeake Bay
  Retriever

MASSACHUSETTS
Bird: Chickadee
Insect: Ladybug

MICHIGAN
Bird: Robin
Fish: Brook Trout

MINNESOTA
Bird: Common Loon

MISSISSIPPI
Bird: Mockingbird

MISSOURI
Bird: Bluebird

MONTANA
Bird: Western Meadowlark

NEBRASKA
Bird: Western Meadowlark
Insect: Honeybee

NEVADA
Bird: Mountain Bluebird
Mammal: Desert Bighorn
  Sheep

NEW HAMPSHIRE
Bird: Purple Finch

NEW JERSEY
Bird: Eastern Goldfinch
Insect: Honeybee
Mammal: Horse

NEW MEXICO
Bird: Roadrunner
Fish: Cutthroat Trout
Mammal: Black Bear

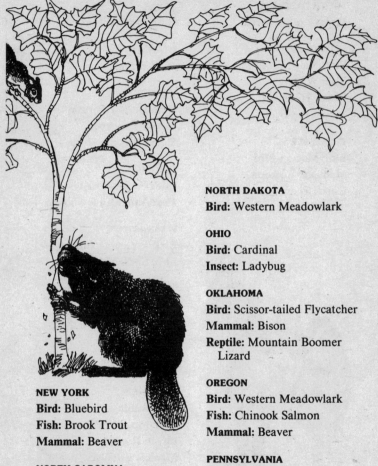

NORTH DAKOTA
Bird: Western Meadowlark

OHIO
Bird: Cardinal
Insect: Ladybug

OKLAHOMA
Bird: Scissor-tailed Flycatcher
Mammal: Bison
Reptile: Mountain Boomer
  Lizard

OREGON
Bird: Western Meadowlark
Fish: Chinook Salmon
Mammal: Beaver

PENNSYLVANIA
Bird: Ruffed Grouse
Dog: Great Dane

RHODE ISLAND
Bird: Rhode Island Red

NEW YORK
Bird: Bluebird
Fish: Brook Trout
Mammal: Beaver

NORTH CAROLINA
Bird: Cardinal
Insect: Honeybee
Mammal: Gray Squirrel
Reptile: Turtle

SOUTH CAROLINA
Bird: Carolina Wren

SOUTH DAKOTA
Bird: Ring-necked Pheasant
Fish: Walleye
Insect: Honeybee
Mammal: Coyote

TENNESSEE
Bird: Mockingbird
Mammal: Raccoon
Horse: Tennessee Walking
  Horse

TEXAS
Bird: Mockingbird

UTAH
Bird: Seagull

VERMONT
Bird: Hermit Thrush
Insect: Honeybee
Horse: Morgan Horse

VIRGINIA
Bird: Cardinal
Dog: American Foxhound

WASHINGTON
Bird: Willow Goldfinch
Fish: Steelhead Trout

WASHINGTON, D.C.
Bird: Wood Thrush

WEST VIRGINIA
Bird: Cardinal
Mammal: Black Bear

WISCONSIN
Bird: Robin
Fish: Muskie (Muskellunge)
Insect: Honeybee
Mammals: Badger, White-
  tailed Deer, Dairy Cow

WYOMING
Bird: Meadowlark

Animal Life Spans

The average human life span is approximately 74.7 years. Below are the average life spans of some other animals.

Animal	Years	Animal	Years
Baboon	20	Elephant (Asian)	40
Bear		Fox (Red)	7
Black	18	Giraffe	10
Grizzly	25	Gorilla	20
Polar	25	Horse	20
Bactrian (two-humped) Camel	12	Kangaroo	7
Cat (domestic)	12	Lion	12
Chimpanzee	20	Pig	10
Chipmunk	6	Rabbit	5
Cow	15	Sheep	12
Deer (White-tailed)	8	Gray Squirrel	10
Elephant (African)	35	Tiger	16

Animal Speeds

THE FAST LANE

The animals below can run faster than humans, who have been clocked at 27.89 miles per hour over an approximate distance of 3/4 of a mile.

Cheetah—70 mph

Pronghorn antelope—61 mph

Lion (charging)—50 mph

Quarter horse—47.5 mph

Elk—45 mph

Coyote—43 mph

Zebra—40 mph

Greyhound—39.35 mph

Rabbit—35 mph

Giraffe—32 mph

Grizzly bear—30 mph

Cat (domestic)—30 mph

THE SLOW LANE

All the animals below move more slowly than humans.

Elephant (charging)— 25 mph

Black Mamba snake— 20 mph

Wild turkey— 15 mph

Squirrel— 12 mph

Pig— 11 mph

Chicken— 9 mph

Spider— 1.17 mph

Giant tortoise— 0.17 mph

Three-toed sloth— 0.15 mph

Garden snail— 0.03 mph

Animal Champions

(Except for two types of bats, the animal champs below are land mammals. See later chapters for other animal champions, like sea creatures and birds.)

LARGEST
African Bush Elephant
  Height: 10 ft., 6 in.
  Weight: 6½ tons

FASTEST
Cheetah
  Speed: 70 mph

SMALLEST
Kitti's Hog-Nosed Bat
  Wing span: 6.29 in.
  Weight: 0.062-0.071 oz.

SLOWEST
Three-toed Sloth
  Speed: 0.15 mph

LONGEST HIBERNATION
Barrow Ground Squirrel
  Length: 9 months of the year

LARGEST BIG CAT
Siberian Tiger
  Length: 10 ft., 4 in.
  Height: 39-42 in.
  Weight: 585 lbs.

TALLEST ANIMAL
  The **giraffe,** which reaches
  a height of 18 ft.

SMALLEST MONKEY

Pigmy Marmoset of South
America
Length: 5½ in.
Weight: 3 oz.

LARGEST KANGAROO

Red Kangaroo
Height: 7 ft.
Weigth: 175 lbs.

FASTEST KANGAROO

**Female Eastern Gray
Kangaroo**
Speed: 40 mph

**LONGEST LEAP BY A
KANGAROO**
42 ft.

LARGEST PET SIBERIAN TIGER

Jaipur, owned by animal train-
er Joan Byron-Marasek of
Clarksburg, N.J.
Length: 10 ft., 11 in.
Weight: 932 lbs.

LARGEST BAT

Bismarck Flying Fox
Wing span: 5-6 ft.

LARGEST GORILLA

Eastern Lowland Gorilla
Height: 5 ft., 9 in.
Weight: 360 lbs.

LONGEST-LIVED

Asian Elephant
Age: 70 years

Is It True—or False?

Turtles can walk out of their shells.

False. A turtle's shell is part of its body. The turtle will die if its shell is removed. Many people think that finding an empty turtle shell on the ground means the turtle has left it to move into a new one. But the empty shell is what remains after a turtle has died.

Rats will desert a sinking ship.

True. Rats, as well as other animals, will try to jump off a sinking ship. This was especially true in the 19th century and earlier, when sail-powered ships were in use. Standards of cleanliness were low, and rats were frequent stowaways. Ship sinkings were also more common.

Elephants are afraid of mice.

False. Mice are found in elephant areas in circuses and zoos, where they sometimes come very close to an elephant's trunk. Some people think elephants fear that mice will run up their trunks. But elephants just ignore the mice.

A frightened ostrich hides its head in the sand.

False. Ostriches sometimes lie down and stretch their necks along the ground when they see an enemy. This makes it more difficult for the enemy to spot them on the African plains. It may look as though the ostrich is sticking its head in the sand, but when an enemy gets too close, the ostrich gets up and runs away. (These largest of all birds are unable to fly.)

Wolves live alone.

False. Wolves live in family groups with parents, mates, cubs, and other relatives, and they hunt in packs. Wolves even take care of old or sick members of the group. The so-called lone wolf is one that has strayed or been driven away from the group.

Popular Pets Around the World

AUSTRALIA

Dogs: Silky terriers, dingoes, cattle dogs (a breed that features a bluish-colored coat).

Other animals: Wombats, platypuses, kangaroos and their young (joeys), wallabies, lambs, emus (a fast-running bird that resemble an ostrich).

AUSTRIA

Dogs: German shepherds, dachshunds, collies, Irish setters, poodles, Labrador retrievers.

Cats: All breeds except Siamese are popular.

Other animals: Cottontail rabbits, guinea pigs, turtles, goldfish, tropical fish.

BRAZIL

Dogs: Most breeds are popular.

Cats: Most breeds are popular.

Other animals: Birds, especially parrots, parakeets, and canaries; turtles, goldfish, hamsters.

CHINA

People in China's cities aren't allowed to have pets, but dogs and cats are sometimes kept as pets on farms. Other farm animals, like cows and horses, are mainly working animals.

DENMARK

Dogs: All breeds, especially cocker spaniels, poodles, and Scottish terriers.

Cats: All breeds.

Other animals: Birds, especially canaries.

ENGLAND

Dogs: Most breeds, including spaniels, Labradors, collies, sheepdogs, Jack Russell and other terriers. In general, large dogs like setters, shepherds, and Great Danes are most popular. About 55 percent of the British people favor purebreds.

Cats: All breeds are popular.

Other animals: Budgie birds (a type of parakeet), hamsters, goldfish.

FRANCE

Dogs: This is a dog-loving country. Big dogs like Great Danes and shepherds are especially popular, but small dogs, such as toy poodles and Shi Tzus, are well liked, too.

Cats: All breeds.

Other animals: Guinea pigs, hamsters, canaries, parakeets.

GREECE

Dogs: All breeds; mixed breeds are favored over purebreds.

Cats: All breeds.

Other animals: Canaries, pigeons, turtles.

IRELAND

Dogs: All breeds, especially Irish setters.

Cats: All breeds.

Other animals: Goldfinches, parrots, canaries, budgies, rabbits, guinea pigs, pet lambs and calves, goldfish.

ISRAEL

Dogs: Many breeds; Canaanite dogs (also called Arab sheepdogs) are especially popular.

Cats: Less popular than dogs.

Other animals: Rabbits.

ITALY

Dogs: All breeds.

Cats: All breeds.

Other animals: Canaries, parrots, pigeons.

JAPAN

Dogs: All breeds.

Cats: All breeds.

Other animals: Lovebirds, macaws, parakeets, goldfish.

MEXICO

Dogs: All breeds.

Cats: All breeds.

Other animals: Parrots, canaries.

SPAIN

Dogs: All breeds are popular, especially the Spanish shepherd.

Cats: All breeds, but less popular than dogs.

Other animals: Canaries, hamsters.

SWEDEN

Dogs: All breeds.

Cats: All breeds.

Other animals: Horses, rabbits, turtles, parakeets, parrots, canaries, tropical fish and goldfish.

SWITZERLAND

Dogs: All breeds.

Cats: Most breeds, except Siamese.

Other animals: Rabbits, baby farm animals, hamsters, canaries, parakeets, goldfish, turtles.

Animal Celebrities

Jack the Baboon

This highly intelligent Chacma baboon belonged to James Wide, a South African railway switchman. Wide was confined to a wheelchair, but he had trained Jack to push him to work, do small chores in the signal box, and finally, to operate the signal levers by himself. Jack's career as a switchman's assistant lasted nine years, until his death in 1890.

Jumbo the Elephant

Jumbo lived for 17 years in the London Zoo, where he reportedly ate 200 pounds of hay and drank five pails of water a day. In 1882 he traveled to New York to appear in P.T. Barnum's circus. Billed as the "largest elephant in or out of captivity," Jumbo was 11 feet tall and weighed 6½ tons. After Jumbo died in 1885, it was estimated that he had given over a million rides to children in his lifetime.

The Monkeys of Helping Hands

Ten years ago, Mary Joan Willard, a behavioral scientist at Boston University, started a program called Helping Hands: Simian Aides for the Disabled. Each monkey in the program is trained to help disabled people by doing such household tasks as taking food from the refrigerator and putting it before its owner; placing a thermos in a holder, opening its lid, and inserting a straw; cleaning up spills; and fetching items. The monkeys come from breeding colonies like the one at Walt Disney World in Orlando, Florida, spend some time in foster homes, and then receive more training before they're ready for their jobs. As of spring, 1988, seven monkeys had been placed with quadriplegics and nearly 70 monkeys were in foster homes across the United States.

Koko and her Kitten

Koko, a female gorilla, lives in the San Francisco Zoo. In 1972, Dr. Francine Patterson, a psychologist, began to teach Koko to communicate by using American Sign Language. Shortly before Koko's twelfth birthday, Dr. Patterson asked the animal what present she wanted, and the gorilla signed "Cat." Koko chose a tailless (Manx) tabby from a litter of kittens and named him All Ball. Koko treated the kitten as if he were her baby. She carried him on her back, tried to tuck him in her thigh, kept him clean, and checked his eyes, ears, and mouth to make sure he was healthy. Koko was very upset when All Ball was run over by a car and killed. Some months later, she "adopted" another kitten—an orange Manx tabby whom she named Lipstick. *Koko's Kitten* and *Koko's Story* are books about Koko, the gorilla.

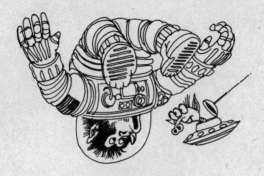

Monkeys in Space

In 1961, the same year astronaut Alan Shepard made the first U.S. manned space flight, two "animalnauts" became space pioneers. Ham and Enos, male chimpanzees, were launched separately into space, where they pulled levers to control their craft. Ham's flight lasted 16½ minutes; Enos completed two orbits of the earth. Both chimps recovered successfully from their flights.

Elsa, the Lioness of *Born Free*

In Kenya, Africa, in the late 1950s, Joy Adamson and her husband George, a game warden, raised an abandoned lion cub, which they named Elsa. The Adamsons brought up the lioness to hunt and to fend for herself, not as a pet in captivity. But even though Elsa was returned to the wild, she had a trusting, affectionate relationship with the Adamsons until her death. The Adamsons even helped to raise Elsa's cubs, Jespah, Gopa, and Little Elsa. Joy Adamson wrote two books about Elsa: *Born Free* and *Living Free. Forever Free* tells the story of Elsa's cubs after Elsa's death. The first two books were also made into movies.

Five Wild Animals as Pets

SKUNKS	They're usually avoided because of the bad-smelling scent they spray when confronted by an enemy, but skunks are basically sweet, good-tempered animals. They can be tamed and trained if they're gotten when young.
OTTERS	These intelligent and curious animals can be trained as pets if they're domesticated at an early age.
OCELOTS	Smaller than most of the big cats, these spotted animals can be tamed, but many become bad-tempered and unreliable.
RACCOONS	Curious and intelligent, they make good pets when they're young, but they tend to become bad-tempered when they get older.
KINKAJOUS	These slender, wooly members of the raccoon family make good pets if they're treated gently. When they become angry or scared, they will bite.

Wild Animals in Your Own Backyard

Do you live in the suburbs of a large city? If you do, then you probably know that these areas are growing larger. This suburban sprawl sometimes spreads into animal habitats. In the Los Angeles area, such wild animals as rattlesnakes, coyotes, cougars, deer, and raccoons are found in suburban neighborhoods. It's against the law to feed these animals, and residents are cautioned not to try to tame them as pets. The Department of Animal Regulation and the Wildlife Waystation, a 160-acre private preserve in the Angeles National Forest, are two organizations that take care of the animals and release them into the wild. So if a deer should stumble up your suburban driveway, call your local vet or humane society and ask whom to contact to send it back to the wild where it belongs.

Animal Words and Phrases

WORD OR PHRASE
As the crow flies

MEANING
The shortest distance between two points

ORIGIN
Crows fly straight to their destination.

WORD OR PHRASE
Bark up the wrong tree

MEANING
Be on the wrong track

ORIGIN
Dogs chase other animals up trees, then stand beneath the tree and bark. Sometimes, they bark up at the wrong tree.

WORD OR PHRASE
Birdbrain

MEANING
A stupid or scatter-brained person

ORIGIN
Birds aren't considered very smart.

WORD OR PHRASE
Bloodhound

MEANING
Someone who's on the trail of something that is lost

ORIGIN
Bloodhounds, bred for tracking, were the first breed whose ancestry or bloodline was traced and for which breeding records were maintained.

WORD OR PHRASE
Dog days

MEANING
The hottest, most humid days of summer

ORIGIN
In Roman times, the hottest weeks in summer were thought to be caused by Sirius, the "dog star," as it rose with the sun.

WORD OR PHRASE
In the doghouse

MEANING
Temporarily out of favor

ORIGIN
In J.M. Barrie's classic story *Peter Pan*, Mr. Darling was rude to Nana, the family dog. He had to spend time in Nana's doghouse as punishment.

WORD OR PHRASE
Laugh like a hyena

MEANING
A wild, crazy laugh

ORIGIN
When excited, a hyena makes a high-pitched, cackling sound.

WORD OR PHRASE
Lion's share

MEANING
The biggest share of something

ORIGIN
Lions take the largest share of the food lionesses have hunted and brought back to the pride.

WORD OR PHRASE
Raining cats and dogs

MEANING
A violent rainstorm

ORIGIN
Long ago, people thought animals had magic powers that could affect the weather. Cats symbolized rain; dogs, windstorms.

WORD OR PHRASE
Smell a rat

MEANING
Suspect something devious is going on

ORIGIN
Cats have the ability to smell rats they cannot see.

WORD OR PHRASE
Two shakes of a lamb's tail

MEANING
Very quickly

ORIGIN
A lamb's tail shakes so briskly, two shakes are over before you know it.

WORD OR PHRASE
Wise as an owl

MEANING
Very wise or smart

ORIGIN
Owls look wise because of their wide-open eyes. They really aren't super-intelligent, but they do have excellent eyesight for hunting by night.

Three Types of Pet Monkeys

Capuchins

Capuchins (called New World monkeys because they come from
the Western Hemisphere) have grasping (holding) tails and are
found in Central and South America. Their natural habitat is
tropical forests. Capuchins can grow up to two feet tall and weigh
as much as four pounds. They're intelligent, friendly, and easily
trained.

Rhesus

Found in Asian forests and rocky hillsides, these Old World monkeys (native to the Eastern Hemisphere) have yellowish-brown fur
and can grow up to two feet tall. These highly intelligent monkeys
are used in scientific experiments. The Rh (rhesus) factor in blood
was named for rhesus monkeys, who share that factor with humans. In the late 1950s, the rhesus was the first animal to rocket
into space.

Marmosets

Long valued as pets, marmosets are tiny New World monkeys.
They can be as small as eight inches or as large as rats. Found in
tropical areas of South America, marmosets are outgoing, friendly
chatterboxes.

Zoos of the World

It's a fact: More people visit zoos each year than go to *all* professional sporting events combined! That's not surprising, really. Just about everyone likes animals, and for most people, a zoo is the best place to see all kinds of animals from around the world "up close and personal." In this chapter you'll find information on U.S. zoos and zoos in other countries, a history of zoos, the Adopt-an-Animal Program, and what animals like lions, tigers, and bears eat each day at one of the world's biggest and best-known zoos.

A History of Zoos

4500 B.C.   Pigeons were kept in captivity in the area of the Middle East that is now Iraq.

2500 B.C.   Elephants were domesticated in parts of India.

1150 B.C.   The Chinese emperor Tanki built a huge marble structure to house a collection of deer.

Around 1000 B.C.   Emperor Wen Wang of China opened a 1500-acre zoo called Ling-Yu—the Garden of Intelligence. At this time, zoos also existed in Egypt and the ancient countries of Babylon and Assyria.

From the 7th Cen. B.C. to the end of the Roman Empire   There were zoos in Ancient Greece. Alexander the Great, the Greek ruler and conquerer, captured many animals on his military expeditions and sent them back to Greece. The Romans maintained zoos and aviaries.

Middle Ages (from about A.D. 500 to 1500)   Large zoos faded out, but European rulers often kept private animal collections.

1519   Explorer Hernan Cortés discovered a zoo in Mexico so large that 300 keepers looked after its collection of birds, mammals, and reptiles.

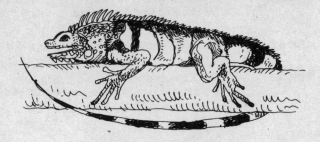

1752   The Imperial Menagerie at Schönbrunn Palace in Vienna, Austria, was founded. Still in existence today, it is considered the first "modern" zoo.

1793   The Jardin Des Plantes (Garden of Plants) was established in Paris, France. It was expanded from a botanical garden to a public zoo.

1828   The London Zoo opened in Regent's Park, London, England.

1872   The Philadelphia Zoo was founded in Philadelphia, Pennsylvania. It is the oldest zoo in the United States.

1890 The National Zoo in Washington, D.C., was established. This is the United States' first and only National Zoo.

1934 The Chicago Zoological Park in Brookfield, Illinois, also known as the Brookfield Zoo, introduced free-view enclosures. This meant animals were separated from visitors by rocks, water, ditches, and dry trenches, instead of by cages and fences. In 1926 this zoo became the first to exhibit a giant panda, named Su-Lin.

1938 The Philadelphia Zoo featured the first children's zoo—called a baby pet zoo—in the United States.

1980s Today, more than 1,000 animal collections all over the world are open to the public.

Zoos Around the World

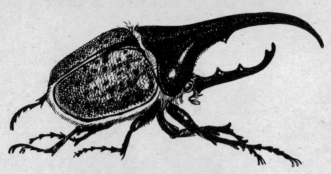

London Zoo—London, England

Set on 34 acres in London's beautiful Regent's Park, this zoo exhibits nearly 8,900 animals. It is especially known for its collection of rare species. Besides such usual zoo animals as giraffes, seals, and polar bears, the zoo includes an insect house, elephant house, deer and antelope house, walk-through aviary, and an animal hospital. The Sobell Pavilion, opened in 1970, houses apes and monkeys (called primates), the lion terraces, giant pandas, and the Zoo Studies Center. The zoo also breeds and exhibits rare animals such as Père David's deer, pigmy hippos, musk-oxen, and Chilean flamingoes.

Paris Zoo—Paris, France

This zoo includes the 16-acre Menagerie du Jardin des Plantes and the 17-acre Parc Zoologique de Paris (Menagerie of the Garden of Plants and the Paris Zoological Park). The Menagerie contains more than 930 specimens of about 275 animal species. Among its more unusual animals are the rare Przewalski's horse, the onager, goral, chamois, and European bison. The Park Zoo in the Forest of Vincennes exhibits its animals in large natural habitats. It contains more than 950 specimens of about 225 animal species, including okapi, giraffes, more than 40 species of antelope, and a number of deer. The Park Zoo also features The Grand Rocher, a 236-foot humanmade mountain with winding paths for wild sheep.

Cologne Zoo—Cologne, Germany

Founded in 1860, the Cologne Zoo occupies 49 acres along the Rhine River. It exhibits about 7,000 specimens of more than 700 animal species. This zoo specializes in apes and monkeys, and it has an excellent aquarium, which also includes reptiles and insects.

Frankfurt Zoo—Frankfurt, Germany

The 19th-century philosopher and animal lover Arthur Schopenhauer helped found this zoo in 1858. Today, the zoo features more than 4,650 specimens of 600 animal species. It was the first zoo in Europe to successfully breed okapi, the black rhino, and the bongo antelope. Twin lowland gorillas were also born here—the only known twin birth of its kind in captivity.

Moscow Zoo—Moscow, U.S.S.R.

Known for its excellent collection of northern animals and exotic species, this 49-acre zoo was founded in 1864. There are small, unbarred enclosures for animals and large paddocks for herds. The Moscow Zoo features 3,000 specimens of 550 animal species.

The Peking Zoo—Peking (Beijing), China

The Empress Dowager Tz'u-hsi founded this 138-acre zoo in 1906. It was originally famous for its collection of rare Asian species. From 1911 to 1949, it was an experimental farm. Its exhibits include an ape and monkey house, elephant house, carnivore enclosure, and an aquatic animal house. Some of the zoo's 4,000 specimens of about 485 species include the rare snub-nosed monkey and white-headed langur (a species of monkey), the kiang (a wild ass), white-lipped deer, the rare takin (a mountain-dwelling species of sheep-oxen), and, of course, the giant panda. The zoo also has a large collection of fish, including some unusual varieties of goldfish. A very rare bird, the white-eared pheasant, was preserved from extinction by the efforts of the Peking Zoo.

Zoos in the U.S.

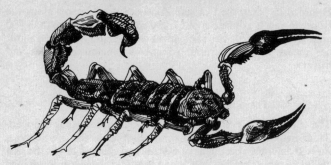

ARIZONA-SONORA DESERT MUSEUM (15 acres)
Route 9
Tucson, Arizona

SPECIAL ATTRACTIONS:
Mountain Habitat, Sonora Desert Exhibit, Aviary

AUDUBON ZOOLOGICAL GARDEN (58 acres)
6500 Magazine St.
New Orleans, Louisiana

SPECIAL ATTRACTIONS:
Asian Domain, World of Primates, Australia exhibit, Louisiana Swamp, Sea Lion Pool

BRONX ZOO (265 acres)
185th St. and Southern Blvd.
Bronx, New York

SPECIAL ATTRACTIONS:
Jungle World, Himalayan Highlands, African Plains, Wild Asia, Childrens' Zoo, World of Birds, World of Darkness, World of Reptiles

BROOKFIELD ZOO · Chicago Zoological Park (204 acres)
3300 Golf Road
Brookfield, Illinois

SPECIAL ATTRACTIONS:
Tropic World, Australian Walkabout, Predator Ecology, Seven Seas Panorama, Dolphinarium

BUFFALO ZOO (23 acres)
Delaware Park
Buffalo, New York

SPECIAL ATTRACTIONS:
Habicat, gorilla habitat,
buffalos, tropical rain forest,
Children's Zoo

CENTRAL PARK ZOO (5.5 acres)
5th Avenue and 64th Street
New York, New York

SPECIAL ATTRACTIONS:
Sea Lion Pool, Tropic Zone,
Temperate Territory, Polar
Circle, Children's Zoo

**CINCINNATI ZOOLOGICAL
GARDENS**
3400 Vine St.
Cincinnati, Ohio

SPECIAL ATTRACTIONS: Cat
House, Insectarium, red pandas, gorillas, Children's Zoo

**CLEVELAND METROPARKS
ZOO** (160 acres)
3900 Brookside Park Dr.
Cleveland, Ohio

SPECIAL ATTRACTIONS:
African Plains, Birds of the
World, Birds of Prey, rhinos,
cheetahs, primates

DALLAS ZOO (50 acres)
Dallas, Texas

SPECIAL ATTRACTIONS:
Okapi, bongo antelope,
Grevy's zebra

THE DARK CONTINENT
Busch Gardens
Busch Blvd. and 40th St.
Tampa, Florida

SPECIAL ATTRACTIONS:
Replica of Africa's Serengeti
Plain, with giraffes, ante-
lope, rhinos in natural settings;
Congo raft trip into jungle

**DENVER ZOOLOGICAL
GARDENS** (76 acres)
City Park
Denver, Colorado

SPECIAL ATTRACTIONS: Bear
Mountain, Feline House,
tropical birds, waterfowl,
hooved animals

DETROIT ZOO (122 acres)
8450 West Ten Mile Road
Royal Oak, Michigan

SPECIAL ATTRACTIONS:
Peguinarium, polar bears,
reptiles, Bird House,
aquarium

**HOUSTON ZOOLOGICAL
GARDENS** (55 acres)
1513 Outerbelt Drive
Houston, Texas

SPECIAL ATTRACTIONS:
Children's Zoo, new large-cat
facility, white tigers,
Discovery Zoo, Tropical
Bird House, Kipp Aquarium

**LINCOLN PARK ZOOLOGICAL
GARDENS** (35 acres)
Stockton Drive at Fullerton Ave.
Chicago, Illinois

SPECIAL ATTRACTIONS:
Large mammal area, Great
Ape House, Farm in the
Zoo, bird walks

LOS ANGELES ZOO
5333 Zoo Drive
Los Angeles, California

SPECIAL ATTRACTIONS:
Koala house, elephant and
camel rides, bird and cat
shows

LOUISVILLE ZOOLOGICAL
GARDEN (73 acres)
1100 Trevilian Way
Louisville, Kentucky

SPECIAL ATTRACTIONS:
African Panorama, MetaZoo
Education Center with indoor
hands-on exhibits, Siberian
tiger, polar bear, and rhino
exhibits, minitrain

MEMPHIS ZOOLOGICAL
GARDEN (36 acres)
2000 Galloway
Memphis, Tennessee

SPECIAL ATTRACTIONS:
Rides, tropical bird house,
waterfowl exhibit, aquarium

MIAMI METROZOO (290 acres)
12400 S.W. 152nd St.
So. Miami, Florida

SPECIAL ATTRACTIONS:
Monorail, cageless exhibits,
African Plains, koalas,
white Bengal tigers, tropical
rain forest, aviary, gorilla
family, free animal shows,
Children's Zoo

MILWAUKEE COUNTY ZOO
(186 acres)
10001 W. Bluemound Rd.
Milwaukee, Wisconsin

SPECIAL ATTRACTIONS:
Zoomobile, penguins, dolphin show

MINNESOTA ZOOLOGICAL
GARDEN
12101 Johnny Cake Ridge Rd.
Apple Valley, Minnesota

SPECIAL ATTRACTIONS:
Tropics Trail, Minnesota
Trail, Japanese macaque
(monkey) exhibit, 1¼-mile
monorail ride, 560,000 gallon Beluga whale tank exhibit,
2 bottle-nosed dolphins

MONKEY JUNGLE
14805 S.W. 216th St.
So. Miami, Florida

SPECIAL ATTRACTIONS:
Continuous shows and exhibits featuring monkeys, apes,
and chimpanzees

NATIONAL ZOO (168 acres)
National Zoological Park
Washington, D.C.

SPECIAL ATTRACTION:
Lion/ tiger complex,
Beaver Valley, giant
pandas, Amazonia/
Aquatics Habitat,
tropical rain forest
coming in 1992

OKLAHOMA CITY ZOO
(110 acres)
2101 N.E. 50th St.
Oklahoma City, Oklahoma

SPECIAL ATTRACTIONS:
Aquaticus Science Park,
tropical birds, Patagonia,
Condor Cliffs, gorillas,
Discovery Theater,
Galapagos Islands exhibit

PARROT JUNGLE
11000 S.W. 57th Ave. at South
Red Rd.
So. Miami, Florida

SPECIAL ATTRACTIONS:
Macaws, cockatoos, parading
flamingoes, baby bird training
area, alligator pond

PHILADELPHIA ZOO (42 acres)
34th and Girard Ave.
Philadelphia, Pennsylvania

SPECIAL ATTRACTIONS:
African Plains, World of
Primates, Treehouse

PHOENIX ZOO (125 acres)
5810 E. Van Buren
Phoenix, Arizona

SPECIAL ATTRACTIONS:
African Veldt, Arabian
oryx, Sumatran tigers, Children's Zoo

RIO GRANDE ZOO (30 acres)
903 10th St. S.W.
Albuquerque, New Mexico

SPECIAL ATTRACTIONS:
Rain forest, reptile house,
polar bears

**RIVERBANKS ZOOLOGICAL
PARK** (50 acres)
**500 Wildlife Parkway
Columbia, South Carolina**

SPECIAL ATTRACTIONS: Penguins, eco-system birdhouse, natural, cageless habitats

**ST. LOUIS ZOOLOGICAL
PARK** (83 acres)
**Forest Park
St. Louis, Missouri**

SPECIAL ATTRACTIONS: Jungle of the Apes, Big Cat Country, Herpetarium, primate house, Cheetah Survival Center, aquatic house, Zooline Railroad, Children's Zoo, animal shows

SAN ANTONIO ZOO (49 acres)
**3903 N. St. Mary's St.
San Antonio, Texas**

SPECIAL ATTRACTIONS:
Monkey Island, Barrier Reef, antelope collection, elephant shows, Children's Zoo Animal Closeups Program, seal and sea lion shows

**SAN DIEGO WILD ANIMAL
PARK** (1800 acres)
**15500 San Pasqual Valley Rd.
Escondido, California**

SPECIAL ATTRACTIONS:
Monorail, mixed species exhibits, Nairobi Village featuring koalas, lowland gorilla, Sumatran tiger, maned wolves, cheetah

SAN DIEGO ZOO (100 acres)
San Diego, California

SPECIAL ATTRACTIONS:
Tiger River, Southeastern
Asian exhibit, Skyfari, koala
habitat, Children's Zoo

SAN FRANCISCO ZOO (65 acres)
Sloat Blvd. at 45th Ave.
San Francisco, California

SPECIAL ATTRACTIONS:
Koala Crossing, Primate
Discovery Center, Gorilla
World, Wolf Woods, Penguin
Island, the only insect zoo
in the Western U.S.

TOLEDO ZOO (30 acres)
2700 Broadway
Toledo, Ohio

SPECIAL ATTRACTIONS:
Hippoquarium, Children's
Zoo, giant pandas

WASHINGTON PARK ZOO
(60 acres)
4001 S.W. Canyon Park Rd.
Portland, Oregon

SPECIAL ATTRACTIONS:
Cascades stream and pond
exhibit, Alaska tundra
exhibit, Penguinarium, polar
bear exhibit

WOODLAND PARK ZOO
(90 acres)
5500 Phinney Ave. N.
Seattle, Washington

SPECIAL ATTRACTIONS:
Natural habitats, African
savanna, gorilla tropical forest, Asian elephant forest, nocturnal house (for animals
active by night)

The "Adopt an Animal" Program

You can adopt a pet zoo animal in your own name or someone else's for as little as $10 (a prairie dog) or as much as $2,000 (a hippopotamus). Your gift helps to feed your adopted animal for one year. You'll get a T-shirt, decal, information about your animal, and an adoption certificate. If you're interested in signing up for the program, write to the zoos below. You can also contact your local zoo to see if they are program members.

Brookfield Zoo
3300 Golf Road
Brookfield, IL 60513

Columbus Zoo
9990 Riverside Drive
Powell, OH 43065

Detroit Zoo
8450 West Ten Mile Road
Royal Oak, MI 48067

St. Louis Zoo
Forest Park
St. Louis, MO 63110

Philadelphia Zoo
34th and Girard Ave.
Philadelphia, PA 19104

Phoenix Zoo
5810 East Van Buren
Phoenix, AZ 85008

Riverbanks Zoological Park
500 Wildlife Parkway
Columbia, SC 29210

Washington Park Zoo
4001 Southwest Canyon Road
Portland, OR 97221

Visiting The Perfect Zoo

WHAT IT'S LIKE TO GO ON A MODERN-DAY AFRICAN SAFARI

Many years ago, people went on safaris in Africa to shoot animals and bring back trophies such as heads, tusks, and skins. Today, it is illegal to kill wild animals in Africa. Animals are protected in national parks and preserves in countries like Kenya and Tanzania. These days, when people go on safari, it's to see animals in the wild—on *their* turf. Below are some of the places you might visit and the animals you would see if you went on an African safari.

Kenya

Tsaro West National Park—Kenya's largest national park, with elephants and herds of antelope, zebras, and giraffes. At Mzima Springs, hippos and crocodiles inhabit freshwater pools.

Amboseli National Park—Near Mt. Kilimanjaro, the tallest mountain in Africa (19,340 feet). Animals include lions, cheetahs, zebras, different kinds of antelopes, and elephants, which sometimes travel in herds of 200 or more.

Aberdare National Park—The lodge at Treetops features a water hole where animals such as rhinos, elephants, buffaloes, lions, and antelopes come to drink, day and night.

Masai Mara National Reserve—Rolling grasslands where you'd find herds of wildebeest, zebras, and gazelles, as well as lions, leopards, cheetahs, and hyenas. Prides of more than 20 lions are often seen here. Along the Mara River are hippo pools.

Tanzania

Lake Manyara National Park—Its most famous inhabitants are tree-climbing lions. Also seen here are streams filled with hippos, a large population of elephants, plus giraffes, baboons, and monkeys.

Serengeti National Park—On the Serengeti Plains. The park features over two million animals, including huge migrating herds of wildebeest, zebras, and gazelles. Other animals seen here include cheetahs, giraffes, lions, leopards, buffaloes, and wild dogs.

For more information on African safaris, contact:

Kenya Tourist Office
424 Madison Avenue
New York, NY 10017
(212) 486-1300

Kenya Tourist Office
9100 Wilshire Boulevard
Doheny Plaza Suite 111
Beverly Hills, CA 90121
(213) 274-6634

Mealtime at the Bronx Zoo

Animals in the wild have to search or hunt for food, but zoo animals are fed carefully prepared diets according to their nutritional needs. Listed here are 10 animals who live at the Bronx Zoo in New York City and what they eat every day.

Camels—Hay, grain

Lions—Ground horsemeat

Capuchin monkeys—Monkey biscuit, green vegetables (kale), a tiny amount of fruit (orange or apple)

Penguins (Magellanic)—Fish

Cleo, the pigmy hippo—Hydroponic grass, grain, hay, apples, carrots

Sloth—Green and yellow vegetables (spinach, kale, yams, carrots)

Giraffe—Hay, grain, browse (tree leaves)

Tigers (Siberian)—Ground horsemeat

Kodiak bears—Dry pellets, fish, chicken necks/backs

Zebra (Grevy's)—Hay, grain, grass

Dogs

Are you thinking about adopting a dog? Do you already have a pet dog? If you love dogs and want to know more about their history, breeds, the basics of dog care, plus advice on where to adopt a dog, then this chapter is for you! And for celebrity-watchers, there's the Dogs' Hall of Fame—all about special dogs that rate superstar status.

A History of Dogs

FAMILY TREE

Miacis

(A long-bodied, short-legged creature that lived about 40 million years ago.)

Tomarctus

(Wolflike animal that lived 10 to 15 million years ago)

Dinictis

(Catlike animal, ancestor of cats)

Canis

(Domestic dogs, wolves, jackals, foxes, coyotes)

From these first domestic dogs came the many breeds we know today—through accidental or selective breeding.

Highlights in the History of Dogs

• Dogs were the first animals who could be trained by humans.

• Early domesticated dogs are thought to have resembled the modern-day dingoes—the Australian wild dogs.

• The African Basenji is one of the oldest known dog breeds. Basenjis, which don't bark, are still used today as hunting dogs in Africa.

• The ancient Egyptians tamed and trained a greyhound-type dog who was an ancestor of the modern day Saluki. This dog was used to hunt antelope.

• The pet dog of one Egyptian pharaoh (ruler) had 2,000 slaves to wait on it.

• The ancient Greeks used dogs to hunt lions in Africa.

• The ancient Romans may have been the first to put dogs into certain categories: horse dogs, shepherd dogs, sporting dogs, war dogs, dogs that follow a trail by scent or sight.

• It was the development of farming that led to the use of dogs to herd and guard livestock.

Dog Breeds

PUREBREDS   Dogs whose parents and ancestors were of the same unmixed breed. These dogs are often expensive to buy and may be entered in dog shows to compete against other purebred dogs.

CROSS-BREEDS   Dogs whose parents were of two different pure breeds. For example, the pups of a cocker spaniel and a poodle are crossbreeds. These dogs are usually given away rather than sold.

MIXED BREEDS   Dogs whose ancestors were a mixture of different breeds. Like crossbreeds, these dogs are usually given away rather than sold. They're sometimes called mongrels, or, informally, mutts.

THE PUREBREDS

The American Kennel Club (AKC) puts purebred dogs into seven groups. A breed is grouped according to its common ancestry, the tasks it was originally bred and trained to perform, or its physical characteristics. These groups, and the breeds that fit into each one, are listed below. Some are popular breeds that are not fully recognized as show dogs by the AKC. Those breeds are marked with a star (*).

HERDING

These dog breeds herd sheep and cattle.

Australian Cattle Dog
Bearded Collie
Belgian Malinois
Belgian Sheepdog
Belgian Tervuren
Bouvier des Flandres
Border Collie*
Cardigan Welsh Corgi

Collie
German Shepherd (also
    considered a working
    dog)
Old English Sheepdog
Pembroke Welsh Corgi
Puli
Shetland Sheepdog

HOUNDS

Hounds are hunting breeds that follow a trail by sound or smell.

Afghan Hound
American Foxhound
Basenji
Basset Hound
Beagle
Black and Tan Coonhound
Bloodhound
Bluetick Hound*
Borzoi
Dachshund
English Foxhound
Greyhound

Harrier
Ibizan Hound
Irish Wolfhound
Italian Greyhound
Norwegian Elkhound
Otter Hound
Pharaoh Hound
Redbone Hound*
Rhodesian Ridgeback
Saluki
Scottish Deerhound
Whippet

TOY

These are the very small dog breeds.

Affenpinscher

American Toy Fox Terrier*

Brussels Griffon

Cavalier King Charles Spaniel*

Chihuahua

Chinese Crested*

English Toy Spaniel

Italian Greyhound

Japanese Chin

Maltese

Manchester Terrier (Toy)

Miniature Bull Terrier*

Miniature Pinscher

Pomeranian

Pug

Shih-Tzu

Silky Terrier

Toy Poodle

Yorkshire Terrier ("Yorkie")

TERRIERS

Terriers were originally trained and bred to dig out rabbits, rodents, and insects from underground burrows since these animals could destroy crops. Terrier comes from the latin word *terra*, meaning "Earth."

Airedale Terrier

American Staffordshire Terrier

Bedlington Terrier

Bull Terrier

Cairn Terrier

Dandie Dinmont Terrier

Fox Terrier

Irish Terrier

Kerry Blue Terrier

Lakeland Terrier

Manchester Terrier

Miniature Schnauzer

Norfolk Terrier

Norwich Terrier

Scottish Terrier ("Scottie")

Sealyham Terrier

Skye Terrier

Soft-Coated Wheaten Terrier

Staffordshire Bull Terrier

West Highland White Terrier

Welsh Terrier

SPORTING

These are hunting breeds that point and retrieve.

American Water Spaniel

Brittany Spaniel

Chesapeake Bay Retriever

Clumber Spaniel

Cocker Spaniel

Curly Coated Spaniel

English Cocker Spaniel

English Setter

English Springer Spaniel

Field Spaniel

Flat-coated Retriever

Finnish Spitz*

German Shorthaired Pointer

German Wirehaired Pointer

Golden Retriever

Gordon Setter

Italian Pointer

Irish Setter

Irish Water Spaniel

Labrador Retriever

Pointer

Sussex Spaniel

Vizsla

Weimaraner

Welsh Springer Spaniel

Wirehaired Pointing Griffon

NONSPORTING

These dog breeds don't fit into the other groups: they aren't hunters, workers, or toys. Nonsporting breeds are raised primarily as pets.

Bichon Frise

Boston Terrier

Bulldog

Chow Chow

Dalmatian

French Bulldog

Keeshond

Lhasa apso

Poodle

Schipperke

Tibetan Spaniel

Tibetan Terrier

WORKING

These dogs serve as guard dogs, watchdogs, guide dogs, police dogs, and sled dogs.

Akita

Alaskan Malamute

American Eskimo*

Austrialian Kelpie*

Bernese Mountain Dog

Boxer

Bull Mastiff

Doberman Pinscher

Giant Schnauzer

Great Dane

Great Pyrenees

Komondor

Kuvasz

Mastiff

Newfoundland

Portuguese Water Dog

Rottweiler

St. Bernard

Samoyed

Shar-Pei*

Siberian Husky

Standard Schnauzer

The History of 24 Popular Breeds

AIREDALE

This terrier, with its rough, wiry coat, originated about 100 years ago in the Valley of Aire in England. Airedales are used to hunt large game in the United States, Canada, Africa, and India. This breed was one of the first to be used for police work.

ALASKAN MALAMUTE

Named for the Alaskan Inuit tribe the Mahlemuts, this handsome arctic sled dog was originally developed to hunt polar bears and wolves and to pull sledges (a kind of sled). It has been used on polar expeditions and for sled dog racing.

BASSET HOUND

This lovable sad-faced dog originally came from France and Belgium and was bred to trail game like deer and rabbits. Bassets are tireless hunters known for their keen sense of smell.

BEAGLE

This popular breed of hound is very old and may have originated in ancient Greece. In England in the late 1500s, people divided hounds into two types—large and small. Beagles were the small hounds that hunted hares. They are known for their large, soft eyes and gentle expressions.

BLOODHOUND

The "detective" dog, known for its wrinkled skin, dignified expression, and excellent tracking ability. This breed goes back to ancient times and may have originated in the countries around the Mediterranean Sea. Bloodhounds made their debut in England around the year 1066.

CAIRN TERRIER

This hardy dog originated in the Isle of Skye, off the coast of Scotland. It was used to root out small game.

CHIHUAHUA

This smooth- or long-haired breed is the smallest and was named for the Mexican state of Chihuahua. Experts think Chihuahuas may have been around since the Toltec civilization in Mexico, about A.D. 900.

CHOW CHOW

This sturdily built, dense-coated breed is one of the most popular. Chows probably originated in China, more than 2,000 years ago. They were once used as all-purpose hunting dogs. Their name comes from the word used by the English to describe cargo they brought from China to England in the 18th century: Chow Chows were part of that cargo.

COCKER SPANIEL

This very popular silky-coated, soft-eyed dog can trace its ancestors back over a hundred years. In England, it was bred and trained to hunt woodcocks (a kind of bird); some experts think the name "cocker" is derived from woodcock.

COLLIE

One of the prettiest and most popular breeds, the collie may have been named for "colleys," the black-face sheep it herded in the Highlands of Scotland. There are two collie varieties—rough and smooth—and both breeds are very old. The long-coated and maned collie of books, TV, and movies is the rough variety.

DACHSHUND

This sturdy, short-legged, long-bodied, quick-moving breed has been around since the 15th century. Dachshund means "badger-hound" in German, and there are three varieties—short-coated, long-haired, and wire-haired.

DALMATIAN

Long known as the mascots and companions of firefighters, the spotted dalmatians were named for the Austrian province of Dalmatia. They were trained to hunt and to run along between the wheels of carriages as companions to the horses. Thus they were also called "coach dogs."

GERMAN SHEPHERD

This intelligent and courageous dog originated in Germany in the late 19th century. Shepherds made their debut in the United States in the early 20th century. German shepherds are hard workers, known as herding dogs, guard dogs, police and army dogs, guide dogs for the blind, and, of course, as loving and loyal pets.

GOLDEN RETRIEVER

Well known as land and water retrievers, and for their beautiful golden coats and gentle natures, Goldens were first developed as a breed in Scotland in the 1860s.

GREAT DANE

This huge, dignified-looking dog has achieved fame as the popular cartoon character *Marmaduke*. Great Danes, which have been around for over 400 years, originated in Germany, where they were bred as working dogs of the mastiff family.

GREYHOUND
This speedy, smooth-coated dog has been bred for thousands of years. Egyptian pharaohs used greyhounds to chase hares and gazelles.

LABRADOR RETRIEVER
This very popular retriever was developed in Newfoundland, Canada, in the late 19th century. Known as excellent water retrievers, "Labs" were once used to bring hooked fish back to fishermen's boats.

LHASA APSO
An ancient dog breed, the long-haired Lhasa may have originated as early as 800 B.C. Its original home was Tibet, where it was prized as a watchdog by the nobility and in monasteries. Lhasas were also thought to bring good luck and to drive away evil spirits.

OLD ENGLISH SHEEPDOG
A shaggy favorite, sheepdogs have been bred for about 150 years. Their heavy blue-gray-and-white coats can hang down almost to the ground.

PEKINGESE
These small (6-9 inches) dogs originated in China around the 8th century. They were considered sacred to Chinese emperors, and the theft of a Pekingese was punishable by death. "Pekes" became popular in England in the 19th century, after British soldiers stole one from the Imperial Palace in Peking and brought it back to Queen Victoria.

POODLE
Whether clipped in a fancy haircut or left shaggy, poodles are popular pets in the United States and some countries in Europe, especially France. Poodles originated in Europe, where they were hunters, herders, and retrievers (they are excellent swimmers).

ST. BERNARD
This huge and powerful breed originated in Switzerland around the first century A.D. St. Bernards were probably descendents of the fighting dogs brought to Switzerland by the conquering Roman armies. St. Bernards were once raised and trained at the Hospice of St. Bernard to rescue travelers lost in the snows of the Swiss Alps.

SCOTTISH TERRIER
Compact, powerful, and wiry-coated, "Scotties" are descendents of the ancient terriers of the Scottish Highlands. Once known as the Aberdeen Terrier, this dog may be one of the oldest British terrier breeds.

YORKSHIRE TERRIER
Long-coated, silky-haired "Yorkies" are lively little dogs named for the English county of Yorkshire. They have been around since about 1860, when they were bred to control rats in the mills and mines. However, they soon became popular as pets.

Dog Champs

THE SIX MOST POPULAR BREEDS

1. Cocker Spaniel
2. Poodle
3. Labrador Retriever
4. Golden Retriever
5. German Shepherd
6. Chow Chow

Rarest

The **Chinook,** a sled dog that originated in New Hampshire about 80 years ago. There are only 76 Chinooks in the United States.

Tallest

The tallest breeds are **Great Danes** and **Irish Wolfhounds.** Both dogs can reach heights of over 39 inches at the shoulder.

Smallest

The smallest breeds are **Yorkshire Terriers, Chihuahuas,** and **Toy Poodles.** Some miniature versions of these dogs have weighed only 16 ounces (one pound) as adults.

Heaviest

The **St. Bernard,** which usually weighs from 150 to 180 pounds. A weight of 310 pounds has been recorded for a St. Bernard.

Fastest

Greyhounds, which have been timed at speeds of up to 40 miles per hour.

Most Valuable

Greyhound racing dogs, which have been valued as high as $250,000.

Six Physical Facts About Dogs

• Dogs have a keen sense of hearing. They can hear sounds that are undetectable to the human ear.

• Chow Chows and Shar-Peis have bluish-black tongues.

• The average life span of a dog is 7 to 15 years, but some dogs live to be 20 years old or even older.

• Depending on the breed, the average size of a litter of puppies ranges from one to ten pups. Occasionally, however, a litter can have as many as 20 pups.

• Female dogs are usually loving and protective mothers, but most male dogs are not very fatherly.

• The saliva of a dog works as an antiseptic and helps to heal wounds.

Dog's Hall of Fame

Barry—The St. Bernard

This canine hero lived at the Hospice of St. Bernard in the Swiss Alps, where his job was to find and rescue travelers lost in the snow. Barry was exceptionally good at his job—in 12 years, he saved the lives of over 40 people. Barry died in 1814 at the age of 14 years.

Bobbie—The Lost Dog Who Found His Way Home

Bobbie, a mongrel who was part Old English sheepdog, became separated from his master while the two were on vacation in Indiana. Somehow, Bobbie had to get back home to Oregon, thousands of miles away on the west coast of the United States. After several false starts, he finally found the right direction. Bobbie had to cross icy rivers, mountains, and deserts on his long journey. After six months of traveling, he made it home.

Igloo—Explorer Dog

This fox terrier was the pet of Admiral Richard Byrd, the famous Arctic and Antarctic explorer. Byrd took Igloo with him when he became the first person to fly over the South Pole (1926) and the North Pole (1928).

Lassie—Popular Canine Character

This brave, loyal, and super-smart collie first appeared in a 1940 book, *Lassie Come Home*. In 1943 the book was made into a movie, followed by several other *Lassie* films. Then came the radio series, which aired from 1947 to 1950. The TV series "Lassie" made its debut in 1954 and was on the air until 1971. Several collies played the part of Lassie on TV.

Laika—Traveler in Space

In 1957 the Soviets launched this female Samoyed husky into space. She was the first "animalnaut" to orbit the earth. At that time, the Soviets had no way of bringing satellites back to earth, so Laika was painlessly put to death by remote control.

Jet—1988 Ken-L-Ration Dog Hero of the Year

Officially named Gridiron's Air Coryell (for the former San Diego Charger coach Don Coryell), Jet is a black-and-tan female Doberman Pinscher. When Jet's owner, a diabetic, fainted, the dog nuzzled the door open, ran to a gate in a four-foot-high fence, opened the latch, and ran to a next-door neighbor's house to summon help. Alerted by Jet's furious barking, the neighbor called 911, and paramedics arrived in time to save the life of Jet's mistress.

Other winners of Ken-L-Ration's Dog Hero of the Year Medal have included a cocker spaniel who saved a three-year-old boy from drowning; a collie who herded 70 goats to safety from a burning barn; a St. Bernard who battled and chased away a grizzly bear; and a miniature poodle who successfully alerted the seven sleeping members of her household to a fire.

Buddy—The First Seeing-Eye Dog

Many blind people have pet dogs that are especially trained to guide and protect them. The first Seeing-Eye dog was a German shepherd named Buddy, who was trained by his owner, Morris Eustis, in Switzerland in 1920.

Baby—The Dog with the Stomach of Steel

Baby, a bull terrier puppy, was brought to the veterinarian by her owner, who thought she wasn't feeling well. When vets operated on Baby, they found that she had swallowed seven quarters, seven dimes, seven nickels, sixty-two pennies, four washers, a nail, a house key, a token, a small piece of wire, and some shotgun pellets. Baby recovered from the experience.

Rin Tin Tin—Canine Movie Star

One of the most popular stars of the 1920s was this German shepherd, whose first movie was *Where the North Begins,* in 1923. He was the first dog to earn over a million dollars.

Rover—The First Canine Movie Star

Rover, a collie, appeared in a 1902 silent film entitled *Rescue by Rover.*

Five Tips on Dealing with Dogs

1. If you meet a strange dog, stand still and let it sniff you. This is how a dog gets to know you.

2. Never reach out to a strange dog, or run away from it.

3. Never take food, bones, or toys from a dog's mouth.

4. Don't bother a dog that has been left in a car or tied up.

5. Be careful when you play with a dog. Even dogs you know very well may bite if they get too excited.

Dogs as Pets

Whether it's a purebred, crossbreed, or mixed breed, a dog can be a wonderful pet. When you adopt a dog, you're getting a true friend who will give you affection, loyalty, and love. When you're feeling sad, your dog will cheer you up; when you're happy, your dog will share your fun. But caring for a pet dog is a responsibility, too. Dogs are sensitive animals who need special attention in order to be happy and healthy. Your dog's whole world revolves around *you!*

Below are some basic guidelines set by the A.S.P.C.A. (American Society for the Prevention of Cruelty to Animals) and other animal experts, which you should follow if you're thinking of adopting a dog, or if you already have a dog.

BEFORE YOU ADOPT YOUR DOG (OR PUPPY)

If you're thinking of adopting a dog, you should first ask yourself these questions:

1. Are you allowed to have dogs where you live (for example, in an apartment building owned by a landlord)?

2. Is your house or apartment big enough for a dog? (A large dog in a small living space usually isn't very happy.)

3. Is there an area outside your house or apartment where you can exercise your dog every day?

4. Are you willing to get up early to walk your dog? Or, if you get a puppy, to spend the time necessary to housebreak it?

5. Can you pay for your dog's food every week?

6. Can you pay veterinarian bills for yearly check-ups, or in case your dog should be sick or injured? (Veterinarians are doctors who specialize in taking care of animals.)

7. Does anyone in your family have animal allergies?

8. Will you be able to live with fur on your furniture, stains on your rugs, a warm body on your bed, and an animal who may be destructive at times? (Dogs, like people, aren't perfect!)

9. How does the rest of your family feel about your having a dog?

10. Will you love and care for your dog every day for the rest of its life?

WHERE TO ADOPT A DOG

(It's always a good idea to have an adult with you when you adopt your dog.)

Animal Shelters

These include dog pounds, animal adoption agencies, and SPCA-type animal societies, and they are the best and cheapest places to get a dog. When you choose a dog from such a facility, you're probably saving it from being put to death due to overcrowded shelters, besides giving it the warm, loving home it deserves. Look in the Yellow Pages under "Animals" or "Animal Shelters" to find the shelter in your city or town. The modest fee paid for the dog may also include shots, neutering, and a certain number of free checkups.

Friends and Neighbors

You may know of someone whose dog has just had a litter of puppies. To find out who in your town might be giving puppies away, check the advertising columns in your local newspaper, or be on the lookout for posters or fliers attached to telephone poles or lampposts, or in stores.

Pet Shops

Many dogs at pet shops come from good local breeders, but others come from "puppy mills" around the United States. These mills breed puppies in inhumane, unhealthy conditions, and the puppies themselves may be unhealthy, or come from unhealthy parents. It's important to find out everything you can about where your puppy or dog came from before you buy it. You'll also probably pay more for a dog at a pet shop than you will at a shelter. Ask the pet shop owner if the shop has a health guarantee.

Breeders

These are the people to go to if you want and can afford to buy a purebred. People who are interested in showing a dog will buy one from a breeder. Before you buy a dog from a breeder, it's important to ask questions about the dog's parents and ancestors and to make sure he or she was bred in a healthful and humane way.

Dog Care—the Basics

EIGHT MUST-HAVES BEFORE YOU BRING YOUR DOG HOME

Pet shops, pet departments in department stores, or stores like Woolworth's are good places to buy much of the pet equipment your dog will need.

1. FOOD
2. FOOD DISH
3. WATER BOWL
4. NYLON OR LEATHER BUCKLE COLLAR
5. LICENSE (from your local shelter or community licensing branch)
6. DOG BRUSH AND COMB
7. TOYS
8. YOUR DOG MUST HAVE HAD ITS SHOTS (from your local shelter or vet)

DIET

Puppies from eight to twelve weeks old need four meals a day. Pups from three to six months old need three meals a day. Six-month-old puppies need to be fed two meals a day. By the time your dog is a year old, one meal a day is enough. Include dry food as well as canned food for a well-balanced diet. Mix dry food with water or broth. Dogs also enjoy such foods as cottage cheese, cooked eggs, and cooked vegetables.

Feed your dog every day and make sure he or she has fresh *clean* water at all times. Wash your dog's dishes often—they must be kept clean for health reasons.

HOUSING

Your dog will need a warm, quiet place to rest. If you don't want to buy a dog bed, you can easily make one out of a cardboard or wooden box. Line your dog's bed with newspapers and an old blanket.

OUTDOOR SHELTERS

The ASPCA and other experts recommend that your dog live inside the house with you. But if, for some reason, your dog can't live with your family and must stay outside, the local ordinances usually require you to have to provide him or her with a proper basic shelter:

1. A wooden dog house with a black tarpaper (weatherproof) roof and sides.

2. The door must be a burlap sack or black rubber mat with vertical slits almost to the top. The entrance must close over to keep your dog's body heat in and cold weather, rain, and snow out.

3. Winter bedding should be made of straw, *never* cloth or rugs (they get soggy and damp and will freeze). Use straw, cedar chips, or newspaper. Change when damp.

4. You'll need a wooden lip at the entrance to keep the bedding inside the house. Otherwise, the bedding could blow away or be kicked outside by your dog.

5. Make sure the house is at least two inches off the ground. That means it needs to be built on four legs (use grained-wood 2 X 4s). This will keep out damp and prevent floor rot.

6. The shelter should be large enough to let your dog stand, turn around, and lie down comfortably, and small enough to let your dog warm the inside with its body heat.

7. Chaining your dog outside is *not* recommended. But if your dog has to be tied up, attach its leash to a metal ring that is attached to a long clothesline, so your dog will have room to move around. Your dog should also be near a shady spot and have food and water available. Do *not* use a choke chain.

Your local hardware store, lumber yard, or do-it-yourself home center should be able to answer any questions you have about building your dog's shelter. Ask parents and/or friends to give you a hand with the building and furnishings, too.

SHELTER DON'TS:

1. Don't tie your dog to a car door handle.

2. Don't use a trash can or metal barrel turned on its side—metal absorbs cold and doesn't retain heat.

3. Don't prop up planks of wood against the side of a building. Chances are they'll collapse.

4. Don't build a leaky dog house.

HANDLING YOUR DOG

Small puppies and little dogs are the easiest to handle; larger breeds, like German shepherds, St. Bernards, or Old English sheepdogs are too big and heavy to lift. If you want or need to carry a dog, pick it up around the stomach. Make sure you support the legs with your other hand.

WALKING YOUR DOG

When you're outside with your dog, *always* keep him or her on a leash. It's the law in most communities. Train your dog to relieve itself in the gutter of the street, *not* on the sidewalk, lawns, parks, or other public places where people walk. Pick up your dog's waste with a pooper-scooper or with newspaper. Dog waste in public places isn't a very pleasant sight for you or other people in your town or city. And the chances are that your community has dog litter laws as well as leash laws.

LICENSES

You'll need to get a license for your dog. By law, all dogs over four months old must be licensed. You can buy a license at an animal shelter. (Your local Town Hall may also have dog licensing procedures.) When you get the license, attach it to your dog's collar. A dog license is also an ID tag, making your dog easier to locate if he or she gets lost.

GROOMING

Most dogs don't need a bath more than two or three times a year. Between baths, help to keep your dog clean and reduce the amount of hair it sheds by brushing and combing it often.

YOUR DOG'S HEALTH AND WELL-BEING

1. Take your dog to the vet for a full check-up and shots once a year.

2. See a vet immediately whenever your dog is sick or injured.

3. Check your dog's collar regularly. As puppies grow, so do their necks, and collars can get too tight and cause wounds and pain.

4. If your dog wears a flea collar, check the dog's neck every day, or every other day. Flea collars can irritate a dog's skin. Flea powders are good alternatives to a flea collar.

5. It's *very* important to have your dog spayed (females) or neutered (males). These simple operations prevent a female dog from having puppies and a male dog from making a female pregnant. The number of stray dogs on the street and in shelters is much too large. There just aren't enough people to adopt all the dogs who need safe loving homes. Neutering your dog will help to keep the canine population down, so that there will be fewer strays. And many experts feel that neutered dogs make better pets.

6. Walk your dog at least three times a day. Dogs need plenty of exercise.

7. See chapter 13 for information on first aid for pets.

TRAINING

Naturally you don't want your dog to jump up on people, bark a lot, or disobey you. It's up to you to teach your dog to be well behaved. The basic commands your dog should learn are "Come," "Stay," "Heel," and "No!" Check your library for books on dog training and obedience, or see if your town has training clubs or classes.

For more information on adopting and caring for a dog, contact your local animal shelter or look for books on the subject at the library.

Dog Names

People have a variety of reasons for choosing a particular name for their dog. Some dogs are named after famous people, favorite places, or things. Others are named for their colors or physical characteristics. Some names are just plain silly. Below are some of the most common and most unusual dog names, according to *Dog Fancy* magazine. The names were sent in by readers of *Dog Fancy* and appeared in its April 1988 issue.

MOST COMMON NAMES

Brandy	Missy	Sam/Sammy
Ginger	Misty	Shadow
Gypsy	Muffin/Muffy	Teddy
Max		

MOST UNUSUAL NAMES

Arctic Flo's Silver Thunder	Redd Cloud Windwalker	Wellington Rathbone
Crash Hanna	Riboflavin Zinc	Yanique Boutique
Master Reflex	Susie-Qs Banana Split	Yankee Poodle
Max-A-Million Bow Dean		

Cats

Did you know that cats were once thought to be evil creatures that could bring bad luck to people? No one believes silly superstitions like that about cats these days, but one thing is for sure—cats are funny, interesting, entertaining animals that make wonderful, lovable pets. Here is just about everything you ever wanted to know about cats and cat breeds, from their earliest history to basic information on adopting and caring for them as pets.

A History of Cats

FAMILY TREE

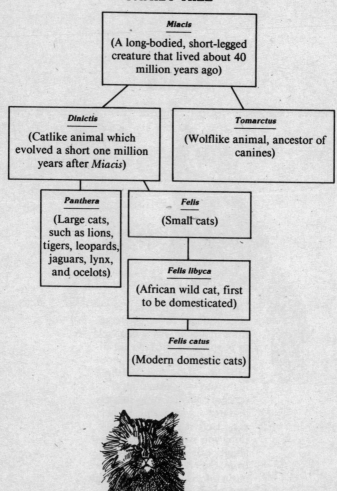

Miacis

(A long-bodied, short-legged creature that lived about 40 million years ago)

Dinictis

(Catlike animal which evolved a short one million years after *Miacis*)

Tomarctus

(Wolflike animal, ancestor of canines)

Panthera

(Large cats, such as lions, tigers, leopards, jaguars, lynx, and ocelots)

Felis

(Small cats)

Felis libyca

(African wild cat, first to be domesticated)

Felis catus

(Modern domestic cats)

Highlights in the History of Cats

• The Egyptians were the first to keep cats in their homes. About 4,000 years ago, they tamed an African wild cat *(Felis libyca)*, which resembled the modern-day Abyssinian breed.

• The Egyptians called domestic cats *miaw* (probably because of the sound a cat makes).

• Cats were highly respected and regarded, partly because they kept granaries free from rodents, like mice and rats. But the Egyptians also thought of feline powers as awesome and mysterious. A cat's glowing eyes were thought to mirror the sun and to protect people from the dark night.

• The Egyptian feline goddess, Bast, was shaped like a cat. Domestic cats were her earthly representatives, and killing a cat was a terrible crime, punishable by death.

• Egyptian cats wore jewels and gold earrings. Fashionable women made up their eyes to look like cats' eyes.

• The Egyptians gave their cats elaborate funerals. The animals were mummified and often buried with mummified mice.

• By 900 B.C., news of the Egyptian cat's ability to control rodents had spread to other countries. Even though it was strictly forbidden to take cats out of Egypt, traders smuggled them onto their ships. By A.D. 100, domestic cats had reached Europe.

• In Europe, during the Middle Ages, cats were thought to be evil and were blamed for everything from spoiling food and drink to causing illness and shipwrecks. People were especially afraid of black cats.

• Even though cats had a bad reputation in Europe, sailors sometimes took them along on sea voyages to keep down the rodent population on ships. Cats made their debut in America in the early 1600s.

• A tabby cat sailed to America with the Pilgrims on the *Mayflower*. Cats were prized as both ratters and pets by the American colonists.

Cats—From Top to Tail

PHYSICAL FACTS ABOUT CATS

EYES

• Vision is a cat's strongest sense.

• Cats can see in almost total darkness. They have a special layer of cells in the retina (called *tapetum*), which acts like a mirror, reflecting any available light back to the cat's eye. This reflected light, known as eyeshine, is what makes a cat's eyes glow in the dark.

• Cats are apparently color-blind. They see images only in shades of gray.

• Like some other animals, cats have a third eyelid, called a nictitating membrane. This membrane helps to protect the eye and can be pale pink or dark in color.

EARS

• Like human ears, cats' ears make it possible for a cat to hear and to keep its balance.

• When cats hear a sound, they often "prick up" their ears. They're aiming their ears to lock onto the source of the sound waves in the air.

• Cats have special nerve endings in their ears that make them more sensitive than humans to high-pitched sounds. Cats can hear noises made by their prey that humans can't hear at all.

NOSE

• A cat's sense of smell is very keen. It can sniff odors that would be totally undetectable to a human.

• A cat's nose can be pale pink, gray, black, or a combination of colors.

WHISKERS

• These coarse hairs contain sensitive nerve endings at the base. The nerve endings are stimulated when the whisker tips brush an object. This helps to guide the cat through tall grass or shrubs when it is stalking its prey.

• Some experts think that a cat's whiskers give the cat information about the amount of room it has when moving through a dark, narrow space. This is thought to be true because a cat's whiskers extend to about the width of its shoulders.

FUR

• A cat's coat is a good insulator and helps the cat adapt to temperature changes. The coat traps a layer of air that insulates the skin. The amount of insulation varies, with shedding of the hair in warm weather and growth of a thicker coat in cold weather.

• Cats who live indoors shed a little hair year round. This is because indoor temperatures are more stable than outdoor, and cats adapt to this stable environment.

• When a cat is approached by a menacing animal, its body and tail fur bristles (stands on end). This helps to make the cat look larger and more threatening.

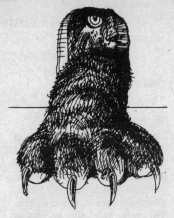

CLAWS

• Cats' claws are used for climbing, hunting, and self-defense. When cats aren't using their claws, they retract them (pull them back) into skin folds above the toe pads. Cats that spend part of their time outdoors should never be declawed: it leaves them almost defenseless.

TAIL

• A cat's tail is an extension of its spinal column. It helps the animal to balance itself while climbing and to right itself during a fall from a height.

• The tail also communicates pleasure or anger to humans or other cats. A softly waving tail means pleasure; frenzied waving or beating the tail on the floor usually means annoyance or anger.

THE PURR

• All cats—domestic and wild—purr, not only when they're contented, but sometimes when they're in pain.

• How cats purr is still a mystery. Many researchers think that purring comes from vibrations in the muscles of the larynx (voice box) and the diaphragm (a muscle used in breathing). Some other experts think that purring is the result of vibrations in a cat's chest, which occur when major blood vessels in that region are stimulated.

BEHAVIOR

• Cats are basically solitary animals. In the wild, they usually hunt and live alone. As pets, cats become attached to their owners and their living space, but they also like to spend time by themselves.

• Most cats are willing to share their homes with other cats or dogs. To keep its independence and sense of territory, the cat will claim its own special spaces away from other animals.

• In a household with more than one cat, there is usually a dominant cat—one who eats and drinks first and gets first choice of places to rest or sleep.

• Cats have an incredible homing instinct. There are many recorded cases of lost or abandoned cats traveling thousands of miles to reach their owners.

• Some animal intelligence tests suggest that cats are smarter than dogs. But cats are proud, independent animals that can't really be trained like dogs. They obey because they're in the mood, or because they like their owners, not always on command.

Cat Breeds

PUREBREDS	Cats whose parents were of the same breed. Purebreds are often expensive to buy and can be entered in cat shows.
MIXED BREEDS	Cats whose ancestors are of mixed breeds, or whose origins are unknown. Mixed breeds are sometimes called "alley cats." They're usually given away rather than sold.

THE PUREBREDS

The cats below are the best known purebreds. They can be registered with the Cat Fanciers' Association, Inc. (CFA).

ABYSSINIAN

HISTORY	Abyssinians probably originated in the African country of Abyssinia (now Ethiopia) thousands of years ago. The cats of ancient Egypt resembled the modern-day Abyssinian. This breed arrived in the United States about 1909.

LOOKS   Abyssinians are short-haired, medium-sized, graceful, and slim. Their almond-shaped eyes are golden or greenish colored; ears and tail are long; the coat is soft and silky. This breed is ruddy, reddish, or bluish in color.

PERSONALITY   This breed is playful, very intelligent, trainable, good-natured, and affectionate. It has a soft melodious voice.

AMERICAN SHORTHAIR

HISTORY   This popular breed arrived in North America in the 1600s and was prized both as a house pet and as a rat and mouse catcher.

LOOKS   The American shorthair includes tabbies (striped), calicos (multicolored), tortoiseshells (red, yellow, and black patches), chinchilla, white, black, blue, red, smoke, cream, and silver colored cats. Shorthairs are muscular, athletic, and healthy, with slighty slanted round, wide eyes.

PERSONALITY   American shorthairs are intelligent, loving, and friendly.

AMERICAN WIREHAIR

HISTORY   The first cat of this breed appeared in a litter of shorthaired farm cats in 1966. It was a red and white male.

LOOKS   This healthy, sturdy breed looks like the American Shorthair, but its hair and whiskers are curly instead of straight.

PERSONALITY   Wirehairs are friendly, affectionate, good-natured, and intelligent.

BALINESE

HISTORY   This longhaired breed was named for the graceful dancers of Bali (an island in the Indian Ocean). Balinese cats in the United States were developed from the longhaired kittens that appeared from time to time in Siamese litters.

LOOKS   These dainty cats are slim, with pointed ears, deep blue almond-shaped eyes, and long silky hair. Like Siamese cats, Balinese colors include seal point, chocolate point, blue point, and lilac point.

PERSONALITY   Balinese are good-natured, affectionate, playful, friendly, very intelligent and trainable. This cat is also fairly "talkative," but its voice isn't quite as shrill as that of its cousin, the Siamese.

BIRMAN

HISTORY   This breed is known as the Sacred Cat of Burma (a country to the north of India). It probably originated centuries ago in Burmese Buddhist temples.

LOOKS   Birmans have long silky hair and a bushy tail; they are stocky and long-bodied. All four paws have white "gloves." Colors include seal point, blue point, chocolate point, and lilac point.

PERSONALITY   Birmans are very affectionate, friendly, playful, quiet-voiced, intelligent, and trainable.

BOMBAY

HISTORY   Bombays originated in 1958, when sable-brown Burmese cats were crossed with black American shorthairs.

LOOKS   These medium-sized, shorthaired cats have large golden or copper-colored eyes and a satiny black coat.

PERSONALITY   Bombays are intelligent, good-natured cats who like attention and companionship. They are also easy to train.

BRITISH SHORTHAIR

HISTORY   This shorthaired breed originated in the late 1800s. Modern-day British shorthairs were developed in the late 1940s, when they were crossed with Persian cats.

LOOKS   British shorthairs are strong, sturdy cats with large round eyes. They are known as good mousers. The breed includes tabbies, tortoiseshells, calicos, smoke, white, black, blue, blue-cream, and bi-color cats.

PERSONALITY   These quiet cats have soft voices and are gentle, easy-going, friendly, intelligent, and devoted.

BURMESE

HISTORY   Most cats of this shorthaired breed are the descendants of a brown female cat from Burma named Wong Mau and a male Siamese cat. Wong Mau was brought to the United States from Rangoon, Burma, in 1903.

LOOKS   Burmese are medium-sized, rounded, muscular cats with large yellow or golden eyes and a shiny, satiny coat. Colors include sable, champagne, blue, and platinum.

PERSONALITY   These cats are sweet and loving, friendly, very intelligent, and easy to train. Burmese are known as the "Teddy Bears" of cats.

CHARTREUX

HISTORY   This breed originated in France in the 1500s. It was bred by French monks.

LOOKS   Chartreux are healthy, hardy, strong cats that resemble the blue British shorthair. They have a medium-short, bluish-gray coat, and large, round coppery or golden colored eyes.

PERSONALITY   Chartreux are good mousers and fearless "watchcats." They are trainable, loving, good-natured, and intelligent.

COLORPOINT SHORTHAIR

HISTORY   This Siamese-type breed originated when Siamese were bred to other types of cats, especially American shorthairs.

LOOKS   Colorpoints are slim and dainty with bright blue almond-shaped eyes. They are similar to Siamese cats, but their points (mask, ears, feet, legs, and tail) are colored differently. Some Colorpoint colors are red point; cream point; seal, chocolate, blue, and lynx point, seal-tortie and chocolate-tortie point; and lilac-cream point.

PERSONALITY   Colorpoints are active, "talkative," sociable, intelligent and easily trained.

CORNISH REX AND DEVON REX

HISTORY　　Both Rex breeds originated in England and were named for the curly-coated Rex rabbit.

LOOKS　　Both Rexes are shorthaired and have slender bodies, long slim legs, and long tails. The Cornish Rex has a small narrow head, oval eyes, high-set ears, and a tight curly coat. Some Cornish coat colors and patterns are white, black, chinchilla, tabby, and calico. Devons have a wedge-shaped head, large wide-set eyes, low-set ears, and a soft wavy coat. Devon coat colors and patterns include white, black, red, chocolate, tabby, tortoiseshell, and calico.

PERSONALITY　　Rexes are affectionate, playful, very intelligent, and trainable.

EGYPTIAN MAU

HISTORY　　*Mau* means cat in Egpytian. This spotted, shorthaired breed originated in Egypt around 1400 B.C. Maus made their debut in Europe in 1950 at a cat show in Rome, Italy. They were then brought to the United States.

LOOKS　　Maus are medium-sized cats with long graceful bodies and slanted green eyes. Colors include silver, bronze, and smoke.

PERSONALITY　　Maus are intelligent, loving, good-natured, active, and playful. They have a soft voice and are moderately vocal.

EXOTIC SHORTHAIR

HISTORY This breed was developed in the 1960s as a cross between a Persian and an American shorthair.

LOOKS Exotic shorthairs are healthy, sturdy-looking cats that resemble Persians. They have round eyes that can be coppery, green, or blue-green in color. This breed comes in a variety of colors and patterns, including white, black, blue, red, chinchilla, tabby, tortoiseshell, calico, and seal, chocolate, and lilac point.

PERSONALITY Exotic shorthairs are good-natured, affectionate, and intelligent and have a quiet, soft voice.

HAVANA BROWN

HISTORY This shorthaired breed got its name because its coat was a rich, deep tobacco color resembling that of a Havana cigar. Havana Browns were developed in the 1950s and are a cross between a seal-point Siamese and a black shorthair.

LOOKS This medium-sized cat is muscular, with a slender tail and oval-shaped bright green eyes. Its whiskers and smooth glossy coat are a rich warm brown color.

PERSONALITY Havanas are good-natured, loving, playful, intelligent and trainable. They are also moderately talkative.

HIMALAYAN

HISTORY

This breed is a cross between a Persian and a Siamese. Himalayans were named for the Himalayan rabbit, which has a similar-patterned coat.

LOOKS

Himalayans are stocky-looking cats with full cheeks, snub noses, and round eyes. They have a long, thick coat. Some Himalayan colors include seal point, chocolate point, blue point, lilac point, tortie point, and seal lynx-point.

PERSONALITY

Himalayans are intelligent, friendly, affectionate, somewhat talkative, and very clean in their habits.

JAPANESE BOBTAIL

HISTORY

This breed originated in Japan, where it has existed for hundreds of years. These cats were thought to bring good luck to their owners.

LOOKS

Bobtails are medium-sized, slender, but muscular cats with short bunny-type tails, high cheekbones, and a medium-length, soft, silky coat. Some colors include white, black, red, tortoiseshell, and *Mi-ke* (pronounced mee-kay), a three-colored coat of black, red, and white.

PERSONALITY

These cats are good-natured, very loving, friendly, and intelligent. They have a gentle voice and are somewhat talkative.

JAVANESE

HISTORY Like the Balinese, this breed was developed as a long-haired version of the Siamese, which it resembles.

LOOKS Javanese are slim, dainty cats with large pointed ears and bright blue almond-shaped eyes. They have silky, long hair. Some Javanese colors include red point, cream point, blue-lynx point, red-lynx point, seal-tortie point, and chocolate-tortie point.

PERSONALITY Javanese are very intelligent, trainable, friendly, good-natured, affectionate, and playful. They are somewhat talkative.

KORAT

HISTORY This ancient breed came from the Korat Plateau in Thailand, where it is also called *Si-Sawat* ("Si" means color; "Sawat" is a wild-growing blue fruit). Korats were thought to bring good luck and were sometimes given as special gifts, but never sold.

LOOKS Korats are muscular, medium-sized cats with heart-shaped heads and large brilliant green eyes. Their glossy coats are a silvery-blue color.

PERSONALITY Korats are affectionate, friendly, good-natured, intelligent, and trainable. They are quiet cats who like a peaceful atmosphere and gentle handling.

MAINE COON

HISTORY This breed is thought to be a cross between Angora cats and a variety of domestic shorthairs. They developed from the cats that were brought to New England by sailors and the early settlers in the 1500s and 1600s.

LOOKS Maine Coons are healthy, sturdily built, muscular cats of medium or large size. They have large round paws, large eyes, a shaggy silky-feeling coat, and a bushy tail. They come in a variety of patterns and colors, including tabby, tortoiseshell, chinchilla, calico, white, blue, black, and cream.

PERSONALITY These cats are intelligent, energetic, playful, gentle, and friendly. Excellent mousers, they are fairly quiet and make soft chirping sounds.

MANX

HISTORY Manx were probably brought to the Isle of Man (off the coast of England, where the islanders are called "Manx") on trading ships from the Orient long ago.

LOOKS Although Manx are well known as tailless cats, some cats of this breed have a short, stumpy tail or even a complete tail. Manx are short-haired, powerful-looking cats with round heads and eyes. Some Manx colors and patterns are white, black, chinchilla, silver, chocolate, lavender, tabby, tortoiseshell, and calico.

PERSONALITY Manx are loving, devoted, playful, friendly, intelligent cats that are somewhat talkative. They are also excellent mousers.

OCICAT

HISTORY This cat was developed as a cross between a chocolate-point Siamese and a part-Abyssinian, part-Siamese. It got its name because the first kitten looked like a baby ocelot (a big spotted wild cat).

LOOKS Ocicats are large, muscular, graceful cats with big almond-shaped eyes and a short glossy coat that is spotted and striped. Ocicat colors include brown-spotted, chocolate, cinnammon, blue, lavender, and silver.

PERSONALITY Ocicats are friendly, intelligent, and trainable.

ORIENTAL SHORTHAIR

HISTORY This breed was develoepd as a cross between a Siamese and other types of shorthairs.

LOOKS These are slim, long-bodied cats with dainty-looking oval paws, large pointed ears, and almond-shaped eyes. Some of the many Oriental patterns and colors are tabby, tortoiseshell, blue, chestnut, cinnamon, ebony, lavender, and white.

PERSONALITY These cats are friendly, talkative, very intelligent, trainable, and fond of attention.

PERSIAN

HISTORY Persian-type longhaired cats were first recorded in Europe in the late 1600s. Modern-day Persians are the descendants of longhaired cats from Persia (now Iran) and Turkish Angora cats. They were brought to England in the late 1800s. Today, Persians are the most popular purebred in the United States.

LOOKS Persians are medium- or large-sized cats with short thick legs, large round paws, a round head and face, and a short thick neck. They have a long thick coat and tail. Some of the over 50 Persian coat colors and patterns include white, black, chocolate, lilac, chinchilla, tabby, tortoiseshell, calico, seal point, chocolate point, and blue-lynx point.

PERSONALITY Persians are quiet, good-natured cats who love to be pampered.

RUSSIAN BLUE

HISTORY The ancestors of this breed may have been blue-coated cats that lived in northern Russia. It is thought that they came to England in the 1860s with Russian sailors. Russian Blues were once known as the Archangel Cat, because the sailors came from the Russian seaport of Archangel.

LOOKS   Russian Blues are graceful cats with long legs, a
long tail, round bright-green eyes, and a short,
bright-blue coat.

PERSONALITY   These cats are easygoing, affectionate, quiet, intelligent, and trainable.

SCOTTISH FOLD

HISTORY   This shorthaired breed descends from a single
folded-eared kitten named Susie who appeared
in a litter of farm cats in Scotland in 1961.

LOOKS   Scottish Folds are sturdy, healthy cats who have
round bodies, paws, heads, and eyes. Their ears
are small and fold down and forward. The ears
look like little caps.

PERSONALITY   These cats are friendly, good-tempered, and
fairly quiet.

SIAMESE

HISTORY   This breed probably originated in Siam (now
Thailand) hundreds of years ago. It's said that
Siamese cats were the royal property of the king

of Siam and were trained to guard the palace by pacing the walls and jumping on the backs of intruders. They were brought to England in 1884, and they arrived in the United States about 1890. Today, Siamese are the second most popular purebreds in the United States.

LOOKS Siamese are slender, short-haired cats with long bodies and legs, dainty oval-shaped paws, and long, thin tails. Their ears are large and pointed, and they have deep blue almond-shaped eyes. Siamese colors are seal point, chocolate point, blue point, and lilac point.

PERSONALITY Siamese are lively, athletic, lovable, very affectionate, intelligent, and trainable. They like a lot of attention and are the most talkative of cat breeds.

SINGAPURA

HISTORY This breed comes from the Asian island of Singapore, and its name means "Singapore" in the Malaysian language. Singapuras made their debut in the United States in 1975.

LOOKS Singapuras are small, stocky, muscular cats with large almond-shaped eyes that can be hazel, green, or yellow in color. They have very short-haired dark-brown-and-ivory-colored coats.

PERSONALITY Singapuras are intelligent, trainable, loving, friendly, and quiet.

SOMALI

HISTORY This breed is a longhaired version of the Abyssinian and was developed from longhaired kittens that appeared in Abyssinian litters.

LOOKS   Somalis are healthy, muscular, graceful cats with green or golden eyes. Coat colors are blue, ruddy, or red.

PERSONALITY   These cats are good-natured, affectionate, friendly, very intelligent, and trainable.

TONKINESE

HISTORY   Tonkinese are a cross between Siamese and Burmese cats. They originated in Canada and the United States in the 1960s and 1970s.

LOOKS   These are medium-sized cats with high cheekbones and almond-shaped blue-green eyes. Their short furry coats are natural mink, champagne mink, blue mink, honey mink, or platinum mink in color.

PERSONALITY   Tonkinese are highly intelligent, trainable, lively, friendly, and very talkative.

TURKISH ANGORA

HISTORY   This is one of the oldest longhaired breeds. Angoras originated in Europe in the 1500s. Their name is derived from the city of Ankara, the capital of Turkey.

LOOKS   Angoras are medium-sized cats with long, graceful bodies, long tails, long pointed ears, and large almond-shaped eyes. They have long silky hair. Some Angora colors and patterns are white, black, blue, black and blue smoke, tabby, tortoiseshell, and calico.

PERSONALITY   These cats are lively, playful, gentle, quiet, very intelligent, and trainable.

FIVE LESS WELL-KNOWN BREEDS

CYMRIC

HISTORY   Also known as a longhaired Manx, this breed was developed in the 1960s. Its name comes from the Welsh word for Wales, *Cymru.*

LOOKS   Cymrics are longhaired, tailless cats that closely resemble Manxes.

PERSONALITY   These cats are loving, friendly, and quiet.

NORWEGIAN FOREST CATS

HISTORY   This hardy breed is centuries old and originated in Norway.

LOOKS   Norwegians resemble Maine Coon Cats, but they have a shaggy two-layered coat. The long topcoat acts as weatherproofing to repel rain and snow.

PERSONALITY   Intelligent and energetic, Norwegians like to be outdoors. They are excellent tree climbers and good mousers.

RAGDOLL

HISTORY   This breed was developed in the late 1960s in California. It was so named because these cats sometimes go limp, like a rag doll, when they're held in one's arms.

LOOKS   Ragdolls are large cats with longish hair that is similar to rabbit fur. Colors and patterns include blue point, chocolate point, seal point, lilac point, and mitted (white mittens on front paws; white boots on hind legs).

PERSONALITY   These cats are intelligent, loving, and very gentle. They will not protect themselves against other cats or dogs and rarely show pain or fear.

SNOWSHOE

HISTORY   This is a new breed, a cross between a Siamese and a bi-colored American shorthair.

LOOKS   Snowshoes are muscular cats with long legs, medium-long tails, large pointed ears, and deep blue eyes. Coat colors are seal point and blue point.

PERSONALITY   These cats are energetic, affectionate, and talkative.

SPHINX

HISTORY   Sometimes called the Canadian Hairless and the Moon Cat, Sphinxes are descended from a hairless kitten born in Canada in 1966.

LOOKS   The Sphinx is a muscular and round-chested cat. Except for some downy hair on its face, the Sphinx is completely hairless. This cat also has no whiskers or eyebrows.

PERSONALITY   Sphinxes are quiet, good-natured cats.

Five Cat Legends and Superstitions

How the Pussy Willow Got Its Name

This legend originated long ago in Poland. A mother cat sat on a river bank crying, because her kittens were drowning. The willows at the river's edge swept their long branches into the water. The branches acted as lifelines, and the kittens were saved. Since then, the buds at the tips of the branches open up every spring. They feel as soft as a kitten's fur.

The Year of the Cat

This occurs every 12 years, according to Chinese astrology (the last time was in 1977). People born in the year of the cat are said to be unselfish, smart, sensitive, and slightly aloof (like a lot of cats!).

The Cat in the Manger

Legend has it that when the newborn baby Jesus lay in his manger, none of the animals around him could soothe him. Then a little tabby cat jumped up next to him and began to purr a lullaby. The baby fell asleep contendedly. Since then, tabbies have featured the letter "M" on their foreheads, as a sign of gratitude from the baby's mother, Mary (also called the Madonna by many Christians).

A Hairy American Superstition

If a young woman living in the Ozark Mountains region can't decide whether or not to marry a certain man, she might "leave it up to the cat." This means wrapping three hairs from a cat's tail in a piece of tissue paper. If the hairs fall into an "N" shape overnight, she'll have her answer—"No."

Cats and Babies

There is no truth to the old belief that cats will try to smother a newborn baby or suck its breath. Cats aren't interested in infants, and apart from an occasional curious glance or sniff, would rather stay far away from them.

Cat Champs

LARGEST POPULATION

The U.S. has the largest cat population in the world—56.2 million, as of 1986.

FATTEST CAT

The average weight of an adult tom (male cat) is 6.2 pounds. Queens (female cats) weigh about 5.4 pounds. An English tabby tom named Joseph tipped the scales at 48 pounds.

HEAVIEST CAT BREED

The Ragdoll, which can weigh up to 20 pounds.

SMALLEST CAT BREED

The Singapura, which has an average weight of 4 pounds (females) and 6 pounds (males).

OLDEST CAT

Cats usually live from 12 to 17 years, but some reach ages of 20 or 21. The oldest cat on record was a female tabby from Devon, England, named Ma. She died in 1957 at the age of 34.

HIGHEST-CLIMBING CAT

In 1950 a four-month-old kitten that belonged to Josephine Aufdenblatten of Geneva, Switzerland, followed climbers to the top of the Matterhorn, a 14,691-foot mountain in the Swiss Alps.

LONGEST-RUNNING FELINE TV SUPERSTAR

Morris, the finicky tabby of TV's Nine Lives commercials, has been advertising cat food since the 1970s.

Famous Cat Lovers

(PEOPLE WHO LOVE CATS ARE CALLED AILUROPHILES.)

Edgar Allen Poe—American Writer (1809-1849)
The writer of such classic horror tales as "The Black Cat" was actually a cat lover. Poe and his wife, Virginia, had a cat named Catarina.

Albert Schweitzer—French Medical Missionary (1875-1965)
Dr. Schweitzer cared for poor patients at his hospital in Africa. He loved all animals, but a favorite pet was a cat named Sizi. The left-handed doctor often wrote out prescriptions with his right hand, because Sizi liked to sleep on his left arm and he didn't want to disturb her.

Robert E. Lee—U.S. General (1807-1870)
Best known as commander of the Confederate armies during the Civil War, Lee had previously served in the U.S. Army during the war with Mexico (1846-1848). During that campaign, Lee wrote to his daughter, Mildred, and asked her to send him a cat to keep him company.

Sir Winston Churchill—British Prime Minister and Statesman (1874-1965)
Churchill's favorite pet during his later years was Jock, a ginger-colored cat. Churchill liked to have Jock eat with him and would often wait until the cat was found before beginning a meal.

Presidents of the United States
Several presidents and their families have been cat fanciers. George Washington and Thomas Jefferson had cats, and Abraham Lincoln owned a cat named Tabby; Rutherford B. Hayes owned the first Siamese cat in the country. Theodore Roosevelt's cat, Slippers, was a polydactl (many-toed) cat. A more recent White House resident was a Siamese named Shan, the pet of President Gerald Ford's daughter, Susan.

Cat Talk

Here is what your healthy cat might be "saying" to you when it purrs, meows, growls, or hisses.

PURRING

"Mmm, don't stop scratching me around my ears and under my chin."

"I love you."

"I'm happy and *very* relaxed."

MEOWING

"I want to go out!"

"Where are *you* going?"

"I want to eat!"

"Water! *Now!*"

"I want whatever *you're* eating (drinking)."

"Who *are* all these guests in *my* house, anyway?"

HISSING, GROWLING, YOWLING

"You're standing on my tail!"

"Ow! Get off my foot!"

"A car trip? No *way!*"

"Stop teasing me. I don't like it!"

"I *warned* you about playing too rough!"

"Dog Alert!"

"Bird ahead."

Cats As Pets

Cats make terrific pets. Whether purebred or mixed breed, they are lovable, will entertain you endlessly, and offer you lots of affection. But cats need plenty of love and affection from you, too. They're more independent than dogs, but they do thrive on your companionship. Cats need lots of TLC (tender loving care) in order to be happy and healthy. Below are some basic guidelines set by the A.S.P.C.A. and other experts, which you should follow if you're thinking of adopting a cat, or if you already have one.

BEFORE YOU ADOPT YOUR CAT (OR KITTEN)

First ask yourself these questions

1. Are you allowed to have cats where you live (for example, in an apartment owned by a landlord)?

2. If you adopt a kitten, are you willing to spend a lot of time with it? (Kittens are baby animals and need special attention and training).

3. Can you pay for your cat's food every week?

4. Can you pay vet bills for yearly check-ups, or in case your cat should get sick or be injured?

5. Is anyone in your family allergic to cats?

6. How does the rest of your family feel about having a cat in the house?

7. Will you love and care for your cat every day for the rest of its life?

WHERE TO ADOPT A CAT

(As with dogs, it's always a good idea to have an adult with you when you adopt a cat.)

Animal Shelters

Shelters are the best and cheapest places to get both cats and dogs. You can often find purebreds at shelters, but chances are you'll fall in love with "your" cat at first sight, whether or not he or she has a pedigree. When you adopt a cat from a shelter, you're giving it the warm loving home it deserves. Check your Yellow Pages for the animal shelter closest to you. Your fee for the cat may include shots, neutering or spaying, and a certain number of free checkups.

Friends or Neighbors

Someone in your town may be giving away a cat or kittens over six weeks old. Ask around, or check newspapers, stores, or lampposts and telephone poles to see if someone is advertising cats or kittens.

Pet Shops

You can buy purebreds at pet shops, but find out if your cat is healthy by making sure its eyes and nose are clean and not watering, and that its ears are clean and free from a wax-like substance that can mean the cat has mites (tiny insects). Examine its fur and skin for fleas, flea eggs, and signs of fungus sores or scabs. Check the litter pan to make sure the cat doesn't have diarrhea. Ask about the number and quality of shots the cat has had, and find out about the shop's health guarantee. You may want to ask your local vet or animal shelter how to tell if the pet shop owner is giving you the right answers about a cat's health.

Breeders

The breeders sell the purest of purebred cats, which may be expensive. As with petshops, you'll need to know everything you can about the cat's health before you buy it.

EIGHT QUESTIONS TO ASK BEFORE ADOPTING OR BUYING A CAT ANYWHERE

1. Is it healthy?

2. Why is it being sold or given away?

3. Has it been checked for worms? If so, when was it checked?

4. Has it been vaccinated? If so, when? When should it be vaccinated again?

5. Has the cat been taking medication? Why, and for how long?

6. If a kitten, how long has it been weaned (no longer dependent on its mother for food)?

7. What times is the cat used to eating?

8. Is there a health guarantee, and how long does it last?

Cat Care—The Basics

SEVEN MUST-HAVES BEFORE YOU BRING YOUR CAT HOME

1. Food (canned and dry food)

2. Shallow food dish and water bowl (Cats don't like to eat or drink out of deep bowls.)

3. Cat collar and I.D. tag (with name and address)

4. Cat toys

5. Cat grooming brush and comb

6. Cat litter and litter box

7. Your cat should have had its shots (from your local shelter or vet)

DIET

Kittens 6 to 12 weeks of age need to be fed 4 times a day; 3 to 6 months, 3 times a day; 6 months to a year, twice a day. Cats one year old and over need to be fed only once or twice a day. Canned and dry cat food provide a balanced diet. Throw away any leftover wet food before each meal. Some cats prefer dry food all the time, just at breakfast, or as a snack. You'll probably have to experiment to see which brand of food your cat likes best. It's also important to give your cat plenty of fresh, clean water. The water dish should be full at all times. Cats do *not* need to drink milk, especially after about the age of 9 months. A steady diet of milk isn't good for cats. Milk makes them fat and gives them diarrhea.

THE LITTER BOX

All indoor cats need a litter box. Good places to put one are the bathroom or back porch. The box should always be kept in the same place (cats like consistency). Clean the box by removing used litter and waste and washing the box. Reline the pan with fresh litter. A cat won't use a messy, smelly litter box.

Kittens have to be taught to visit the litter box after each meal. After they eat, kittens usually groom themselves; then they look for a place to relieve themselves. The litter box should be nearby, so that kittens will learn to recognize it and eventually be able to find it for themselves.

HOUSING

Cats like to nap, and they need warm, dry places to sleep. Old clean towels and blankets are good cat beds, but your may cat prefer to sleep on *your* bed, on a chair, on a rug, or under the sofa. Some cats pick one spot and always sleep there; others like to try out new places to snooze.

It's safer to keep your cat in the house. Unlike dogs, they don't need to go outside. Outdoor cats can get hit by cars, lost, hurt in fights, or poisoned. If you must let your cat go out, make sure he or she is wearing a stretchable collar with an I.D. tag (rigid collars are dangerous if they get caught on a fence post or tree branch). Young kittens should *never* go outside. Also, don't leave your cat alone in a room with an open window.

HANDLING YOUR CAT

To pick up your cat, place one hand under its front legs and the other under its hind legs. Lift gently. *Never* pick up a cat by the scruff of the neck (behind the ears).

GROOMING YOUR CAT

Cats are clean animals that groom themselves. They usually don't need baths, but they do need to be brushed and combed. Brushing helps keep your cat's fur clean and reduces the amount of shedding. It can also reduce hairballs—hair a cat swallows when licking itself clean.

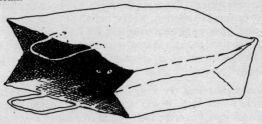

CAT TOYS

Kittens and cats are very playful and curious. You can buy cat toys or make your own. Your cat will probably like a cardboard box or a paper bag to hide in. Many cats enjoy pouncing on and tearing up sheets of newspaper or tissue paper (the kind found in gift boxes). Crumple up a piece of aluminum foil and let your cat chase it. Attach a piece of string to a doorknob and let it hang. Your cat will enjoy batting at it.

For more information on adopting and caring for a pet cat or kitten, contact your local animal shelter, or look for books on the subject at the library.

YOUR CAT'S HEALTH AND WELL-BEING

1. Take your cat to the vet once a year for a checkup and shots. Contact a vet immediately if your cat is injured or seems sick.

2. Check your cat's ears every so often for mites and check its body for sores or cuts.

3. Absolutely, positively have your cat neutered (male) or spayed (female). This simple operation makes it impossible for your cat to have kittens. There are too many stray cats and kittens on the streets and in shelters. Sadly, not all of them can or will be adopted. Spaying or neutering will not hurt your cat or change its personality; the fact is that your spayed or neutered cat will live a longer, healthier life. Neutering or spaying should be done soon after your cat is about six or seven months old.

4. If your cat has fleas, try using flea powder. Flea collars can hurt the skin on its neck. If you must use a flea collar, check your cat's neck every so often for signs of irritation. And make sure the collar is loose enough to slip over his head if it gets caught on something.

5. *Don't* have your cat declawed—it's like removing the fingernails of a human being. Cats do need to sharpen their claws and often choose a chair, sofa, or rug to scratch. You can keep your cat from clawing furniture by providing it with a scratching post, or a small rug. A firm, sharp "No!" every time your cat starts to claw furniture will let him or her know this is not acceptable behavior. It may take awhile, but your cat will finally get the message. You can also have your vet trim your cat's claws regularly, or ask him or her how to do it yourself.

6. See page 270 for information on first aid for pets.

Thirteen Plants that Are Poisonous to Cats

Most cats like to eat grass and plants. But the following plants are poisonous, and cats should be kept away from them. It's important to know exactly what kind of plants you have in your house, apartment, or yard.

Plant	Poisonous Part
Bittersweet	Bark, leaves, and seeds
Dumb cane (also called Dieffenbachia)	All parts
Poison hemlock	All parts
Ivy, English and Baltic	Berries and leaves
Jimsonweed (thorn apple)	All parts (*extremely* poisonous)
Marigold/marsh marigold	All parts
Mistletoe	White berries
Oleander	All parts (*extremely* poisonous)
Philodendron	All parts
Poinsettia	All parts
Poison ivy	All parts
Potato	Unripe tubers, sprouts from tubers
Rhubarb	The leaf blades

MORE ABOUT POISONS

Cats are curious animals who will sometimes sniff and possibly drink liquids that are not good for them. Over-the-counter drugs are not good for cats either. Listed below are 10 substances cats should never swallow or be exposed to:

Aspirin

Cod liver oil

Vitamins intended for people or dogs

A diet heavy in liver (contains Vitamin A, too much of which is not good for cats)

Iodine, Idoform, and gentian violet (used to disinfect wounds in humans)

Turpentine (can be absorbed through the skin)

Insect sprays

Plant sprays

Antifreeze (cats are attracted by its sweet taste)

Mothballs, pine tar, paraffin (wax)

For more information on substances that are poisonous to cats contact your local Humane Society or vet.

Cat Names

If you can't decide what to name your new cat or kitten, you might consider the names below. They are among the most popular, according to *Cat Fancy* magaine. These names were sent in by *Cat Fancy* readers and appeared in the magazine's February 1988 issue. Starred names(*) are used for both male and female cats.

Male		*Female*	
Smokey(ie)*	Samson	Samantha	Annie
Tiger*	Sylvester	Misty	Baby*
Max	Blackie	Muffin	Callie
Charlie	Lucky*	Fluffy*	Lucy
Rocky	Morris	Patches	Pyewacket*
Tigger*	Sebastian	Punkin*	Angel
Sam/Sammy*	Tuffy*	Missy	Cleopatra
Mickey*	Amadeus	Smokey*	Katie
Toby	Pepper*	Tabitha	Shadow*
George	Casper	Tigger*	Tiffany

CAT FANCY'S 24 MOST UNUSUAL NAMES

Cat Fancy readers also sent in these interesting names, which appeared in the February 1988 issue of *Cat Fancy* magazine.

Abbie Normal	Donut Downs	Pouncival
Aggi-tator	Elvis Purrsley	Purrcilla
Amtrak	Ginnyrator	Robert Redfurred
Bugsy Malone	Jennyfur	Shedwina
Catillac	J. R. Mewing	Tiedye
Cheetoes	Katsper	T-Bone Tom
Cleocatra	Mikhail Gorbachat	Warren Peace
Dandy Lion	Opus No. One	Vanilla

Horses

If you like horses and want to know more about them, then you've turned to the right chapter. You'll find fascinating facts on the history of horses, their personalities, looks, and breeds. Plus famous horses; the biggest, tallest, and smallest horse; and explanations of those special words and phrases used by people who own, ride—or just plain love—horses.

A History of Horses

FAMILY TREE

> **Eohippus**
>
> (A dog-sized creature that lived 40 to 60 million years ago. Also known as the "dawn horse.")

> **Orohippus, Epihippus, Mesohippus, Miohippus, Parahippus, Merychippus**
>
> (A variety of small horselike creatures that lived throughout prehistoric eras in the earth's history.)

> **Pliohippus**
>
> (A horse that emerged in the Pliocene era—10 to 1 million years B.C. The ancestor of the modern horse.)

> **Equus Caballus**
>
> (Closest direct ancestor of the modern horse. *Caballus* emerged in the Pleistocene era, also known as the Ice Age—1 million to 8150 B.C.)

Highlights in the History of Horses

• During the Ice Age, herds of horses roamed every continent except Antarctica. But sometime during this era, horses mysteriously vanished from North America. One theory explaining their disappearance is that the horses migrated north and west to Siberia across a land bridge.

• The people who lived in central Asia around 4000 B.C. were the first to tame and ride horses.

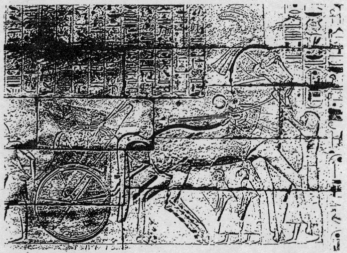

• The ancient Egyptians captured and trained horses to pull chariots into battle.

• The Hittites, ancient peoples who lived in Asia Minor and Syria, wrote detailed manuals in cuneiform (a system of writing using symbols as words) about horse care.

• About 400 B.C., the ancient Greeks developed basic rules for horsemanship (riding and handling horses). These rules are still in use today.

• Horses were bred for size and stamina during the Middle Ages. They carried knights and heavy equipment into battle and wore armor, like their riders.

• In A.D. 1519, horses reappeared in North America. They were brought to Mexico by the invading Spanish *conquistadores* (conquerors).

• Native Americans used horses for hunting and fighting. Horses played an important part in the colonizing and settling of America from the 1600s well into the 1800s. They were used for transportation, individually, and as teams for stagecoaches and covered wagons; for clearing land and plowing; and (briefly) as mounts for Pony Express riders who carried the mail between St. Joseph, Missouri, and Sacramento, California.

• Today, horses are kept for riding, hunting, competitive sports like racing and polo, and as performers, in circuses, rodeos, and movies. Show horses are specially trained for jumping and other show events.

Horses—From Head to Hoof

When you come across the words *pastern*, *forelock*, and *withers*, do you know which part of a horse's body they refer to? Whether you ride horses or just like to read about them, you'll want to know the special names for the body parts of a horse:

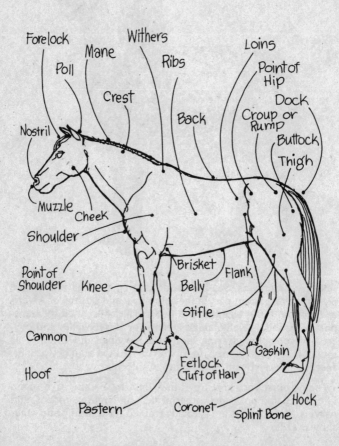

A Roundup of Horse Facts

• There are about 75 million horses in the world.

• A horse's height is measured in *hands*. One hand equals about four inches.

• Horses come in three basic sizes:

Heavy draft—The largest breeds, used for load hauling and farm work

Light—Breeds used for riding, jumping, and showing

Pony—Any small horse that is under 14.2 hands (58 inches) high. Some ponies are only 26 inches high. Ponies are known for their hardiness and often serve as childrens' mounts and pets.

• Horses in the wild run in herds. The herd is headed by a stallion (mature male) and includes mares (mature females), foals, and colts.

• Foals—baby horses—are born with their eyes open. They can stand up almost immediately after birth and are able to run around within a few hours.

• A foal usually inherits its father's (sire's) looks, but its mother's (dam's) personality and constitution.

• A year-old colt (young male horse) is half-grown. Colts reach their full height and weight at five years old. A filly is a female horse that is under four years old.

• The average lifespan of a horse is 20 years, but some horses live for 30 or even 40 years.

• Horses have a keen sense of smell, hearing, and direction. Their skin is sensitive and will respond to the lightest touch.

• Nonracing horses usually cannot run faster than 36 miles per hour.

• Horses are vegetarians. They eat mainly grass and, in winter, hay. Horses also enjoy special feeds of oats, nuts, bran, carrots, sugar beet pulp, and barley. Small, whole apples, apple slices, and an occasional sugar cube are favorite treats.

Horse Breeds

There are over 250 different breeds of horses throughout the world. Horse breeds are classified into three types: *hot bloods* (highstrung, fiery, fast horses of Oriental or Eastern origin), *cold bloods* (the easygoing heavy draft horses), and *warm bloods* (mixtures or crosses of hot and cold bloods, often show jumpers and other competition horses).

Below is a roundup of some of the best-known horse breeds.

LIGHT HORSES

ALBINO
(Also known as the American Cream)

HISTORY: The Albino originated in Nebraska in 1937. It is thought to be a descendant of a stallion named Old King, who was sired by an Arab stallion out of a Morgan mare.

LOOKS: The average height of an Albino is 15.1 hands: average weight is 1,100 - 1,145 pounds. Coat colors include ivory white with an ivory or lighterwhite mane, blue eyes, and pink skin; cream with a darker cream mane, cinnamon-colored skin, and dark eyes; cream, with a cream-colored mane, blue eyes, and pink skin.

PERSONALITY AND USE: Albinos are obedient horses that are easy to train. They are used for riding.

AMERICAN SADDLEBRED

(Also known as the Kentucky Saddlebred, the Saddler, and the American Saddlehorse)

HISTORY: The Saddlebred originated in Kentucky in the early 1800s, where it was developed as a cross between the English Thoroughbred, Morgan, and Narragansett Pacer.

LOOKS: This breed stands 15 - 16 hands high. Coat colors are bay (reddish-brown), black, chestnut (various shades of brown), gray, or roan (a solid color sprinkled with white hairs throughout).

PERSONALITY AND USE: Saddlebreds are intelligent, gentle, and quiet but energetic. They are riding and show horses, and were once used for light draft work.

ANDALUSIAN

HISTORY: The Andalusian originated in Spain. It is probably a descendant of the Barb (from the Barbary States) and Arabian horses brought to Spain in the 8th century during the Moorish invasion. (The Moors were nomadic people of Northern Africa.) The original Andalusians interbred with a variety of horses and influenced many European breeds. Andalusians traveled with Christopher Columbus across the Atlantic on his second voyage. Today, Andalusians are usually found in Europe and South America.

LOOKS: This breed stands 15.1 - 15.3 hands high and weighs about 1,250 pounds. Coat colors include gray, bay, black, chestnut, or roan.

PERSONALITY AND USE: Andalusians are steady, energetic horses used for pleasure riding. They are also known as good jumpers.

APPALOOSA

HISTORY: Appaloosas descended from the horses that were brought to America by the Spanish *conquistadores* in the 1500s. Their name comes from the Palouse River, which runs through Washington and Idaho. This territory was once the home of the Nez Percé Indians, who were the first to breed the Appaloosa selectively.

LOOKS: This breed stands 14.1 - 15.1 hands high and weighs 880-1,280 pounds. Appaloosas have spotted coats called snowflake, leopard, frost, marble, spotted blanket, or white blanket.

PERSONALITY AND USE: Appaloosas are obedient and quiet, but lively. Used as riding horses, they move quickly and gracefully.

ARAB

(Also called Arabian)

HISTORY: The elegant Arab is the aristocrat of horses. One of the oldest breeds, the Arab originated in Saudi Arabia sometime before 3,000 B.C. Because of its beauty, speed, and endurance, it has been bred with other horses, especially the English Thoroughbred, to improve breeds or to create new breeds.

LOOKS: Arabs are long-necked, straight-backed, muscular horses that stand 14 - 15 hands high and weigh 840 - 990 pounds. Coat colors are gray, bay, chestnut, black, or roan.

PERSONALITY AND USE: Arabs are gentle, but spirited and high-strung. They are used as riding horses and sometimes for light draft work.

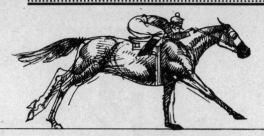

ENGLISH THOROUGHBRED

HISTORY: The Thoroughbred originated in England in the early 1700s. All Thoroughbreds, past and present, are the descendants of three Arab stallions who were imported to England from Middle Eastern countries.

LOOKS: This elegant, long-necked racing horse is generally considered the most beautiful breed in the world. Thoroughbreds stand 14.3 - 17 hands high and weigh 705 - 990 pounds. Coat colors are bay, dark bay, black, chestnut, and gray. White markings are often seen on the head and legs.

PERSONALITY AND USE: Thoroughbreds are intelligent, highstrung, energetic horses known for their speed and stamina. They are used for racing and riding.

IRISH HUNTER

HISTORY: The sure-footed Irish Hunter originated in Ireland and is a cross between the English Thoroughbred and the Irish Draft Horse.

LOOKS: This breed stands 16 - 17.1 hands high. Coat colors include bay, brown, black, gray, or chestnut.

PERSONALITY AND USE: Irish Hunters are obedient, quiet horses. They are used as riding horses, hunters, show jumpers, and in other horse show events.

LIPIZZANER

HISTORY: The best-known members of this breed are the world-famous, highly trained "dancing" stallions of the Spanish Riding School of Vienna, founded in 1729. Here the Lipizzaners are taught to perform beautiful and often difficult feats of equitation, such as prancing, turning, and circling; the *levade,* wherein the forelegs are lifted high into the air; and the *capriole,* in which the horse jumps up in place with all four legs off the ground and kicks out with the hind legs before landing.

Lipizzaners are descended from Spanish and Italian stock imported into Austria in the 1500s. They were named for the village of Lipizza (today situated in Yugoslavia). Today, Lipizzaners are raised in Austria, Yugoslavia, Italy, and Hungary.

LOOKS: Lipizzaners stand 15 - 16.1 hands high. Their coats are usually gray, but are sometimes bay, black, roan, or white.

PERSONALITY AND USE: These are patient, willing, and intelligent horses, used primarily as riding and harness horses and sometimes for draft and farm work.

MORGAN

HISTORY: This sturdy breed is descended from a small bay stallion, Justin Morgan, foaled in Massachusetts in 1790. He was named for his second owner, Thomas Justin Morgan. The Morgan horse gained a reputation for being unbeatable in the weight-pulling competitions of the day. It was also once used in trotting races.

LOOKS: Morgans are elegant horses that stand 14 - 15.1 hands high and weigh 800 - 1,000 pounds. Coat colors are bay, chestnut, or black, often with white markings.

PERSONALITY AND USE: The Morgan is obedient and energetic, a fast horse with a lot of stamina. Morgans are used for riding and for light draft work.

MUSTANG

HISTORY: The name Mustang comes from the Spanish word *mestengo,* which means "wild." Mustangs are descendants of the Andalusians and Arab Barbs brought to the New World by the Spanish explorers. Nomadic native Americans of the Great Plains captured and kept Mustangs as mounts, but many of the horses escaped and formed wild herds. Vast numbers of wild Mustangs roamed the western states until the beginning of the 20th century. Since then, they have been hunted down from a population of two million to a few thousand, protected in horse sanctuaries on government land and on ranches. It is a federal offense to kill wild horses, but as of 1988, the law protecting them was being questioned.

LOOKS: Mustangs are long-maned, sturdy-looking horses that stand 14 - 15 hands high. They have a wide variety of coat colors, including palomino (golden-gray), dun (yellowish-gray), and mouse-colored.

PERSONALITY AND USE: Mustangs are strong, courageous horses that have a lot of stamina. Used for riding, they are independent and can be difficult to train.

PALOMINO

HISTORY: Palominos were probably brought to the New World by the Spanish explorers in the 1500s. They were bred by early Mexican breeders and were discovered by North Americans during the Mexican-American War of 1846 - 1848. Today, Palominos are popular as riding, parade, and show horses.

LOOKS: Palominos stand 14 - 16 hands high and weigh 1,100 - 1,145 pounds. Their beautiful coats are golden-colored, and they have white markings on their faces and lower legs. A palomino's mane is either lighter or darker than its coat, and its eyes are dark or hazel.

PERSONALITY AND USE: Used as riding horses, Palominos are quiet, obedient, and easy to train. They are often good jumpers.

PINTO

HISTORY: Native Americans captured these spotted horses from the Spanish *conquistadores* of the 16th century. Pintos were also ridden by the buffalo hunters of the Great Plains and the cowboys of the "Old West."

LOOKS: The sturdy-looking Pinto stands 14.1 - 15.1 hands high. There are two coat types: **overa,** with white patches on a colored background, and **to-biano,** with variously colored patches on a white background.

PERSONALITY AND USE: Pintos are obedient, quiet horses that are used for riding and for light draft work.

QUARTER HORSE

HISTORY: This fast-moving breed originated in Virginia and the Carolinas, where it was developed by the early settlers. Originally a cross between Australian and English horses, quarter horses were named for the spirited races they ran down the main street of a village for a distance of a quarter-mile.

LOOKS: Quarter horses stand 14.1 - 16 hands high and average 940 - 1,210 pounds. Coat colors include chestnut, bay, brown, black, dun, red dun, buckskin, palomino, gray, blue roan, or red roan.

PERSONALITY AND USE: Quarter horses are even-tempered, obedient, and lively. They move quickly and gracefully and are used for riding and sprint (short-distance) racing.

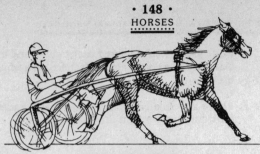

STANDARDBRED

HISTORY: Standardbreds are descended from an English Thoroughbred stallion named Messenger, who was brought to the United States in the late 1780s. Standardbreds became important as pacing and trotting racehorses.

LOOKS: This breed stands 14.1 - 16.1 hands high and weighs 790 - 1,170 pounds. Coat colors include bay, brown, black, chestnut, sometimes gray or roan.

PERSONALITY AND USE: Standardbreds are lively, competitive horses that are easy to train. Because of their great speed, they are used most often as pacing and trotting horses.

TENNESSEE WALKING HORSE

HISTORY: This breed originated in the United States in 1886 and is descended from Black Allan, a crossbred Morgan and Hambletonian stallion. The present-day Tennessee Walking Horse is also part English Thoroughbred, Standardbred, and Canadian Pacer. Its name comes from its unusually fast, four-beat "running walk."

LOOKS: Walkers stand 15 - 16 hands high. Coat colors are black, bay, brown, chestnut, gray, or roan.

PERSONALITY AND USE: These horses are quiet, obedient, sociable, and energetic. They are used as riding horses.

HEAVY DRAFT HORSES

CLYDESDALE

HISTORY: The muscular Clydesdale originated in Scotland in the 1700s. It was used to haul coal and for farm work, and later as a carriage horse.

LOOKS: The strongly built, hardy Clydesdale stands 16 - 17 hand high and weighs 1,540 - 2,200 pounds. Coat colors are bay, brown, chestnut, or roan. Anheuser-Busch uses a team of Clydesdales in its advertising.

PERSONALITY AND USE: These are calm, sociable horses that are used for heavy draft and farm work.

ENGLISH SHIRE

HISTORY: Shires are said to descend from the Great Horse, a type of charger used in jousting tournaments in medieval England. They were used as carriage horses and to pull early horse-drawn buses.

LOOKS: This breed is the tallest and heaviest in the world. Shires stand from 16.1 - 17.3 hands high and weigh 1,760 - 2,200 pounds. Coat colors are bay, brown, black, chestnut, or gray, often with white markings.

PERSONALITY AND USE: Shires are good-natured, obedient horses with a great deal of strength and stamina. They are used for heavy draft and farm work.

PONIES

ASSATEAGUE AND CHINCOTEAGUE

HISTORY: These wild ponies are probably the descendants of a group of horses that survived a shipwreck in early colonial times. Their name comes from the islands off the coast of Maryland and Virginia, where they live.

LOOKS: Assateague and Chincoteague ponies stand about 12 hands high. Many have pinto (spotted) coats, but all coat colors are seen.

PERSONALITY AND USE: These ponies are independent and stubborn. Their life in the wild has enabled them to stand up to harsh weather conditions. Tamed, they are used for riding and for light draft work.

FALABELLA

HISTORY: Falabellas, the smallest ponies in the world, were first bred by the Falabella family on their ranch in Argentina. Their most direct ancestor is the Shetland pony. They are found in Argentina, the United States, Canada, and Great Britain.

LOOKS: This tiny breed may stand 3 - 10 hands (12 - 40 inches) high. Coats come in a variety of colors, but Appaloosa-type coats are favored by breeders.

PERSONALITY AND USE: Falabellas are graceful, intelligent, quiet ponies, strong for their size, and used for riding and light draft work. They are popular as pets, especially in North America.

PONY OF THE AMERICAS

HISTORY: This breed originated in the United States in 1956 and is descended from a miniature half-Shetland, half-Appaloosa stallion named Black Hand.

LOOKS: These ponies stand 11.1 - 13.1 hands high. Coat colors are the same as those of the Appaloosa.

PERSONALITY AND USE: These are quiet, obedient ponies, versatile, fast, and good jumpers. They are popular as riding ponies and racers, and are often used for pony trekking.

SHETLAND

HISTORY: This pony breed is found all over the world. It originated in the Orkney and Shetland Islands of Scotland, perhaps as far back as the Bronze Age (about 3,500 B.C.). However, some experts claim that Shetlands are descended from horses brought to the Scottish islands by ships of the Spanish Armada (naval fleet) in 1588. In the 1800s, Shetlands were used as "pit ponies" to haul coal in British mines.

LOOKS: Shetlands stand 9 - 10 hands high and weigh 330 - 400 pounds. Coat colors are usually pie-bald (black with white spots), skewbald (spotted with white or any color except black), chestnut, bay, or black.

PERSONALITY AND USE: These ponies are strong, hardy, and lively, but not always obedient. They are used for riding, to pull light carts, and for light farm work.

Horse Champs

HEAVIEST BREED
The **English Shire,** a heavy draft and farm horse.
Height: 16.1 - 17.3 hands (5 ft., 4 in. - 5 ft., 8 in.)
Weight: 1,760 - 2,200 lbs.

LARGEST AND HEAVIEST HORSE
Brooklyn Supreme, Belgian stallion who lived in Ogden, Iowa, from 1928 to 1948.
Height: 19.2 hands (6 ft., 6 in.)
Weight: 3,200 lbs.

TALLEST HORSE
An English Shire named **Sampson** (renamed Mammoth), who lived in Bedfordshire, England, in the 1800s.
Height: 21.2½ hands (7 ft., 2½ in.)

SMALLEST BREED
The **Falabella** of Argentina.
Height: 3 - 10 hands (12 - 40 in.)
Weight: 80 - 100 lbs.

SMALLEST HORSE
Little Pumpkin, a stallion foaled in 1973 in Inman, South Carolina.
Height: 3.5 hands (14 in.)
Weight: 20 lbs.

OLDEST HORSE
Old Billy, a cross between a Cleveland and an Eastern Blood. **Old Billy** died in England in 1822 at the age of 62.

OLDEST THOROUGHBRED RACEHORSE
"Tango Duke," a bay gelding (neutered male) who died in Barongarook, Australia, in 1978 at the age of 42.

Horses' Hall of Fame

Algonquin—White House Horse

This pony was the pet of President Theodore Roosevelt's son, Archie. When Archie caught the measles, Algonquin was smuggled into the White House to cheer up the sick child. Algonquin was the first—and probably the only—horse ever to visit the inside of the White House.

Bucephalus—Famous Horse of a Great Ruler

Bucephalus belonged to the ancient Greek ruler and conquerer Alexander the Great. Bucephalus was legendary for his incredible speed, and for the amazing deeds he could perform as Alexander's mount. Bucephalus died in 326 B.C. after the battle of the Hydaspes River. Alexander honored his horse by founding the city of Bucephala on the banks of the river.

Comanche—Sole Survivor of a Terrible Battle

This cavalry horse was the only survivor of the Battle of Little Big Horn in 1876. During this battle, the 7th Cavalry of the U.S. Army, led by the reckless General George Custer, fought the Sioux Indian tribe at Little Big Horn, Montana. The battle is often called Custer's Last Stand. The entire company perished, except for Comanche. The horse suffered seven wounds, some of them serious, but he recovered and lived to be 30 years old.

Incitatus—Pampered Horse of a Cruel Emperor

Incitatus belonged to Caligula, emperor of ancient Rome from A.D. 37 to 41. Caligula was one of the most ruthless rulers in history, but he loved Incitatus and treated him royally. The mentally unbalanced emperor made the horse a consul (government official) of the Roman Empire and housed him in a marble stable with an ivory stall, a gold drinking goblet, and a staff of slaves.

Justin Morgan—Father of a New Horse Breed

A new breed, the Morgan horse, was named for Justin Morgan. A small bay stallion foaled in 1790 in Massachusetts and named for his second owner, Thomas Justin Morgan, this was the first horse for whom a new breed was named. He was valued for his great intelligence, strength, and speed.

Marengo-War Horse

This white Arabian stallion was the favorite horse of the French emperor Napoleon Bonaparte. Marengo carried Napoleon into many battles and was wounded eight times. After the emperor's last battle, at Waterloo, Belgium, in 1815, Marengo was taken as a prize of war by the British. He is depicted in several famous paintings, and his skeleton can be seen at the National Army Museum in London, England.

Moifaa—Survivor of a Shipwreck
In 1904 this eight-year-old New Zealand racehorse was on a
ship bound for England. The ship sank in a storm, and Moifaa
almost drowned, but he was washed ashore on a desert island.
The horse roamed the island for almost two weeks before he
was rescued and sent on to England. There he competed in the
Grand National Steeplechase. Moifaa won the race by eight
lengths in 9 minutes, 59 seconds.

Muhamed—Equine Math Whiz
Muhamed lived in Germany in the late 1800s. He was owned
by Karl Krall, who trained him to do math problems. After four
months of training, Muhamed, blindfolded by a sack (to prove
his master wasn't helping him), could calculate cube roots. He
could also add, subtract, multiply, and divide. Muhamed would
give the answer to a math problem—say, 25—by tapping his left
hoof twice, his right hoof five times. Scientists were never able
to prove that Muhamed's prowess was the result of trickery.

Horses' Personalities and Behavior

• Like humans, individual horses show different personality traits. They can be lazy, generous, aggressive, nervous, easygoing, curious, obedient, or stubborn.

• Horses can sometimes act "skittish" (nervous or highstrung). One reason for their skittishness is that they can look backward with one eye and forward with the other simultaneously. Thus, they can see people, other animals, and vehicles coming and going.

• A frightened horse will often kick or bite, but its usual reaction to extreme danger is to *bolt* (run away).

• Horses are very intelligent. They are basically good-natured animals, especially if they trust their handlers. But a horse that has been cruelly treated will react to the person who abused it with fright for a long time.

• Horses communicate by *whinnying* and *neighing*. The whinny is a short, low, sad sound that signals distress. The neigh is a loud, drawn-out sound that signals a variety of feelings:

Long, high-pitched repeated neigh—well-being and contentment

Short, high-pitched neigh—anger

Short, low-pitched neigh—fear.

• The position of a horse's ears also gives clues to its mood:

Both ears laid back flat—The horse is ready to rebel or attack.

Ears twitching backward, first one, then the other—anger

One ear laid back and the other forward while the horse is being ridden—tension and possible unwillingness to obey the rider's commands.

Ears that barely move, together with a movement of the head—insecurity and fear

Drooping ears—passivity

Both ears bent slightly forward while the horse is moving—security and well-being.

• Most horses are friendly and sociable toward other animals. They sometimes have a stable companion such as a dog, a cat, or even a kid goat. The racehorse Diamond Jubilee had a cat companion who accompanied him to races.

• Horses rub noses with each other as a sign of friendship.

Gaits

The way a horse moves forward is called its *gait,* of which there are five basic types:

1. **The Walk** This is a slow gait of four beats, in which the horse moves its legs one at a time in the following order: right hind leg, left foreleg, left hind leg, right foreleg.

2. **The Trot** This is a slightly faster, springing gait of two beats, in which the legs move diagonally in pairs: the right foreleg moves with the left hind leg; then the left foreleg moves with the right hind leg; or vice versa.

3. **The Canter** This is a fast gait of three beats. First one hind leg moves, then the other hind leg together with the diagonally opposite foreleg, then the other foreleg.

4. **The Pace** This is a springing gait of two beats, in which the legs on the same side of the body move together, first on one side, then on the other.

5. **The Gallop** This gait resembles the canter, but is faster and not as smooth.

Coat Colors of Horses

SINGLE-COLORED COATS

White

Black

Chestnut—yellow to red

TWO-COLORED COATS

Red Roan—white and red or yellow

Gray—white and black

Yellow dun—dark yellow, black points (legs)

Dun—yellow to the knees and hocks, then black, mane and tail are black

Blue dun—silver, black points, mane, and tail

Bay—reddish, black points, mane, and tail

THREE-COLORED COATS

Roan—white, black, and red

PATCHED-COATED HORSES

Piebald—large black-and-white patches

Skewbald—patches of white and any other color except black

Odd-colored—large patches of more than two colors

Head Markings

Star—A white mark on the head which can be of any shape and various sizes.

Stripe—A narrow white mark which runs down the face from the forehead, between the eyes, to the nostrils.

Blaze—A broad splash of white which covers much of the forehead between the eyes and runs down the nose to the muzzle.

White muzzle—A white mark which covers one or both lips up to the nostrils.

White face—A large white mark which covers the front of the face from the forehead to the muzzle.

Horse Terms

BASIC EQUIPMENT
(Words in italics are defined later in the list)

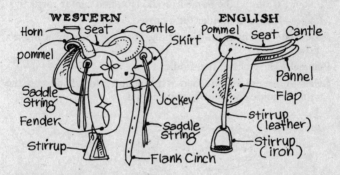

Bit—The steel end of a *bridle* that is fitted into the horse's mouth. The most common type of bit is the snaffle.

Bridle—Headgear with which a horse is controlled, including the bit and the *reins*.

Breastplate—A piece of equipment attached to the *saddle* to keep it from slipping back.

Browband—A narrow part of the bridle that fits into the *headpiece*. The browband goes in front of the horse's ears and is used to keep the headpiece from slipping.

Cantle—The back of the saddle.

Cavalletti—A grid of heavy poles laid on the ground and used to train horses to jump.

Cavesson—The simplest type of *noseband;* also a specially made, rugged headcollar used in *lunging*.

Cheekpieces or Cheekstraps—Straps that buckle on either side of the bridle. They are adjusted to make sure the bit lies just at the corners of the horse's mouth.

Clenches—The pointed ends of shoeing nails that penetrate the horse's hooves after it has been shod.

Halter—Part of the bridle that circles the head and throat. A lead line is often attached to the halter.

Headpiece or Crownpiece—A strap on the bridle that fits over the horse's head behind the ears. It is connected to the cheekpieces.

Lunge line or rein—A line connected to the halter and used in *lunging* (training the horse to walk, trot, and canter correctly).

Manger—Raised container for a horse's food.

Noseband—The band on the bridge that goes around a horse's nose.

Pommel—The front of the saddle.

Reins—A line or lines attached to the bit and bridle. Riders use the reins to guide and control their horses.

Saddle—The leather seat on which the rider sits. The saddle is attached to a girth—straps that encircle a horse's body and help to keep the saddle in place.

Stirrups—Iron rings attached to either side of the saddle to hold the rider's feet.

Surcingle—A wide belt, band, or girth that encircles a horse's body. Surcingles keep saddles, packs, or rugs in place.

Tack—Riding equipment. "Tack up" means to put on the saddle and bridle.

Throatlatch—The long thin strap on the bridle that goes under the throat and buckles on the left side. The throatlatch keeps the bridle from slipping over the horse's head in case of an accident.

GROOMING EQUIPMENT

Body brush—Removes dust, dirt, and grease from the coat. Also used to brush the mane and the tail.

Curry comb—A rubber or plastic comb used to remove caked mud from horses that have been outside.

Dandy brush—Used to brush off dry mud and sweat from a horse's coat.

Hoof oil and brush—These prevent brittleness of the horn (the hard part of the hoof).

Hoof pick—Used to clean out a horse's hoof.

Mane comb—A comb used to groom the mane.

Sponges—Used to wipe a horse's eyes, nose, and dock.

Stable rubbing cloth—A cloth used to polish the horse's coat.

Tail bandage—Used to flatten and smooth out the tail hairs.

Water brush—A brush used to flatten the mane and tail before braiding or bandaging.

OTHER TERMS

Action—The way in which a horse moves.

Aids—Signals the rider communicates to a horse by using his or her hands, legs, seat, and voice.

Combined system—One in which a horse is kept in a stable at night and turned outside in a paddock (an enclosed area of pasture) by day, or vice versa.

Crib biting—Restless activity in which a stabled horse bites its manger, door, or other nearby object and sucks wind (air) at the same time.

Head carriage—The position of a horse's head.

H.H.—The abbreviation for "hands high."

Lateral movements—Sideways movements.

Nap—A stubborn or bad-tempered horse that refuses to obey its rider.

Under saddle—Being ridden.

Unschooled—Untrained.

Weaving—This happens when a nervous horse shifts its weight from one foot to another and weaves its head back and forth over the lower part of the stable door.

Horses and You

Have you always wanted to own your own horse? If you have, you share that dream with a lot of other kids (and many adults, too). But horses are expensive pets. Besides the cost of the horse itself (say, $1,000), you need a place to house it—a good-sized yard with room for a shelter, if you keep your horse at home. Or the money to board it at a stable (about $50 a month), if lack of space or zoning laws require it. Hay and feed for your horse will cost about $3 a day. Then there's the cost of equipment, shoeing, vet fees, insurance, and saddle repairs.

If you can't afford your own horse, but you really want to be around horses, you might consider taking riding lessons at a local stable, riding school, or club (check the Yellow Pages). Some stables might eventually let you help out with the horses as well.

Adopting a Wild Horse

One way to own a horse is to adopt one of the wild horses that roam on open government land. There are too many horses crowded into wilderness areas that are shrinking because of real estate development. The government is trying to find good homes for these horses. To adopt a wild horse, you must prove that you have enough space for it, that you won't try to make money from the animal, and that you can have it moved from its holding corral to your home. The cost of adopting a wild horse is about $125. To find out more about wild horse adoption, write:

> Adopt-A-Horse Program
> Bureau of Land Management
> P.O. Box 25047
> Denver, CO 80225

> or

> The International Society for the
> Protection of Mustangs and Burros
> 11790 Deodar Way
> Reno, NV 89506

Farm Animals

Do you know how many cattle there are in the world? Or why a chicken named Weirdo is one of the world's chicken champs? Which farmyard favorite will follow you around and can be led on a leash—just like a dog? The answers to these questions, plus many other facts, can be found in this chapter on the Big Five of farm animals—cattle, chickens, goats, pigs, and sheep.

Cattle

HIGHLIGHTS IN THE HISTORY OF CATTLE

• Cattle originated millions of years ago in India. By the early Pleistocene era, they had migrated to Europe, North Africa, and the rest of Asia. Cattle belong to the ox family, like the bison, yak, and water buffalo.

• An early species of long-horned cattle, the *aurochs,* was hunted by people during the Stone Age. Cave drawings of the *aurochs* have survived from 30,000 B.C., and it was first domesticated around 10,000 B.C.

• The ancient Egyptians worshipped the bull-god Apis. Because of their belief that cattle were sacred, the Egyptians raised the animals in luxury and let them die of old age rather than killing them for food.

• Long-horned cattle traveled with Christopher Columbus to the New World, landing in the West Indies in 1493. In 1624 the Pilgrims imported cattle to New England.

• American pioneers used steers (neutered bulls) to pull covered wagons and plows. Steers were slower than horses, but they stood the heat better and didn't need as much water.

CATTLE FACTS

• There are almost 1,200 million cattle in the world. The United States has about 180 million. India has over 176 million, but India also has the lowest consumption of beef, because cows are considered sacred by Indians who practice the Hindu religion.

• Cattle stand about five feet tall and weigh from 1,000 to 2,000 lbs. Their average lifespan is 15 years, although some live up to 30 years.

• Cattle are ruminants—mammals whose stomachs have four sections. After they swallow their food, it is mixed and softened in the first two chambers of the stomach. Then it returns to the mouth as a ball called the "cud," which is rechewed thoroughly. The food is then reswallowed and passes through the first two stomach sections into the third, where moisture is squeezed out. The fourth chamber actually digests the food through the action of gastric juices.

• Most dairy cows can give milk for five or six years, but some produce milk for 20 years or more.

• There are 277 cattle breeds. Major beef cattle breeds include Angus, Hereford, Shorthorn, and Charolais. Some major dairy cow breeds are Ayrshire, Holstein-Friesian, Guernsey, and Jersey.

CATTLE CHAMPS

Heaviest

A Holstein-Durham cross named Mount Katahdin, who lived in Maine in the early 1900s. He weighed 5,000 pounds.

Most Milk Given

A Holstein-Friesian from California gave 465,224 pounds of milk during her lifetime (1964 - 84).

Most Expensive Cow

Mist, a Holstein, was brought for $1.3 million at a cattle auction in Vermont in 1985.

Most Expensive Bull

Joe's Pride, a Beefalo (3/8 bison, 3/8 Charolais, 1/4 Hereford), was sold for $2,500,000 in 1974.

Chickens

HIGHLIGHTS IN THE HISTORY OF CHICKENS

• The founding father of chickens (and all birds) is the *archaeopteryx* (ar-kee-op-ter-ix), a crow-sized, feathered flying animal with a reptilelike body and claw-tipped wings. The archaeopteryx lived about 145 million years ago.

• The chicken's most direct ancestor is the wild red jungle fowl of Thailand, Burma, Sumatra, and eastern India.

• Chickens were probably the first domesticated birds. They were tamed about 5,000 years ago.

• By 1400 B.C., the Chinese were raising chickens for meat and eggs. Soon after, chickens were exported to Egypt. They were also raised in Ancient Rome and Greece.

• In A.D. 43, chickens were brought to England by the Roman invaders.

• Chickens made their debut in North and South America in the 1500s. They were introduced there by the Spanish explorers.

• Chickens boarded the *Mayflower* with the Pilgrims to cross the Atlantic and then traveled westward with the American pioneers.

• Over the centuries some chickens have been used as show animals and as family pets.

CHICKEN FACTS

• Chickens can't really fly; at best, they can flap a few feet off the ground.

• Chickens have a keen sense of hearing and good eyesight, but poorly developed senses of taste and smell.

• It takes 21 days for a chicken egg to hatch. Chicks are nourished in the egg by the yolk. When a chick is about to hatch, it chirps faintly, then chips its way out of the shell with its beak. A newly hatched chick bonds with (remembers) its mother. It can run around a few hours after birth.

• Mother hens shelter their chicks under their wings. They scratch up food, including grain, worms, and insects, for their chicks to eat.

• The average weight of a rooster (a male chicken, also called a cock) is 6 to 13 pounds; hens weigh 4 to 10 pounds. A bantam (miniature chicken) can weigh less than 1½ pounds.

• Most chickens have four clawed toes on each foot. One breed, the Dorking, has five.

• Hens lay about 240 eggs a year. A pullet (a hen less than a year old) starts to lay eggs at about five months old.

• Chickens that are kept in coops and allowed to mingle with other chickens have a "pecking order," whereby they peck each other to determine which will eat or drink first. Even the smallest chick will fight for its place in the pecking order.

• Chicken breeds include the White Leghorn—the most popular breed of egg layer in the country—the Black Orpington, Rhode Island Red, Rhode Island White, Red Rock, Plymouth Rock, and White Sully.

• Chickens are the only domestic fowl that have combs—fleshy growths that stand up on the tops of their heads. There are seven types of combs: rose, strawberry, single, cushion, buttercup, pen, and V-shaped.

CHICKEN CHAMPIONS

Best Egg-Laying Breed

The White Leghorn, which can lay up to 300 eggs a year. One White Leghorn laid 371 eggs in 364 days at the College of Agriculture, University of Missouri, in 1979.

Heaviest

Weirdo, a 22-pound White Sully, who lived in Calaveras County, California.

Longest Flying Distance

A bantam named Sheena flew 630 feet, 2 inches, in 1985 in Parkesburg, Pennsylvania.

Largest Egg

A New Jersey White Leghorn laid a 16-ounce egg in 1956. The egg had a double yolk and a double shell.

Largest Chicken Ranch

The Croton Egg Farm, in Croton, Ohio, has 4.8 million hens that lay about 3.7 million eggs each day.

Goats

HIGHLIGHTS IN THE HISTORY OF GOATS

• Most domestic goat breeds probably descended from the bezoar, also called the pasang, a wild goat that lived in Persia (now Iran). The bezoar is still found in the mountains of southwestern Asia.

• Goats were first domesticated about 9,000 years ago, probably in southwestern Asia.

• Through the centuries, goats have been bred for food (milk, cheese, meat) and for their hair (wool) and hide, from which leather is made. They are used as work animals in some countries, such as India.

GOAT FACTS

• There are more than 400 million goats worldwide. The United States has about 3 million goats.

• Goats range in height from about 16 inches (miniature goats) to 40 inches. Goats can weigh anywhere from 44 to 250 pounds. Some goats have horns and a pointed chin beard (from which we derive the word "goatee").

• The lifespan of a goat ranges from 8 to 18 years.

• Like cattle and sheep, goats are ruminants (see "Cattle Facts" earlier in this chapter).

They eat alfalfa, or a commercially prepared feed like Sweet Feed—a combination of oats, corn, and grains. They like carrots and apples as treats. Goats also graze on grass and other plants. They like lots of clean, fresh water to drink.

• Goats have a well-developed sense of taste. They are attracted by salty-tasting things, such as paper, and they like to lick the salt off people's hands. They are known for rooting out almost anything containing minerals and chewing on it.

• Butting (hitting the head against something) is a goat's way of greeting other goats. They also butt at trees, gates, or fences for fun, and they will butt at people or things to show anger. Unlike horses, goats don't kick in displays of aggression.

• Goats are good runners and excellent climbers.

• Domestic goats are intelligent and doglike in their behavior. They can be trained to a leash and like to follow their owners around. Historically, they have been used as beasts of burden, to pull carts, and as pets, in addition to their roles as farm animals.

GOAT BREEDS

There are over 200 breeds and varieties of domestic goats. Listed below are some of the best known breeds.

ANGORA
This white-faced, small-bodied, thick-fleeced goat is a source of wool. Angora are found in Turkey, South Africa, and the United States. They like mild dry climates. Both the nanny goat or doe (female) and the billy goat or buck (male) have horns.

CASHMERE (KASHMIRI)
This is a small-bodied, white-faced, long-haired goat with large ears and small horns. The undercoat is woven into the highly prized and expensive wool called Cashmere. Cashmeres are also kept for milk and meat. They live in mountainous areas of China and Iran, and the Kashmir area of India and Pakistan. Both does and bucks have beards.

FRENCH-ALPINE
Alpines are short-haired goats with large bodies and medium-sized ears that stand up straight. They are dairy goats, found in Switzerland, France, and the United States.

NUBIAN
This short-haired dairy goat has a multicolored coat, long legs, long, drooping ears, and a large nose. Some are horned. Nubians live in India, the Middle East, North Africa, Great Britain, and the United States.

SAANEN
The Saanen originated in the Saanen Valley of Switzerland and was introduced into the United States. This large, short-haired dairy goat has a white or cream-colored coat and may be horned. Both does and bucks may have beards.

TOGGENBURG
The Toggenburg is an important dairy breed. It originated in the Toggenburg Valley of Switzerland and is now found in Great Britain and the United States as well. This small goat has a light-to-dark-brown coat and white markings on its face, ears, tail, and lower legs.

Pigs

HIGHLIGHTS IN THE HISTORY OF PIGS

• Wild pigs originated in Europe about 40 million years ago. They were in Africa and Asia about 25 million years ago.

• Present-day domestic pigs are probably descended from two wild pig types—the European wild boar and the East Indian pig.

• Pigs were first domesticated in China nearly 7,000 years ago.

• Pigs made their debut in the New World in the 1400s and 1500s. They were introduced by such explorers as Christopher Columbus and Hernan de Soto. Some pigs from the de Soto expedition were left with Native American tribes; others wandered off and became wild. The razorback hog of the southeastern United States is thought to be a descendant of these wild pigs.

• Through the centuries, pigs have been used for food and in the making of medicines. Their skin and hair have been used for leather goods and bristle brushes.

PIG CHAMPS

FATTEST PIG
The fattest pig on record was Big Bill, a Poland-China hog that weighed 2,552 pounds. He measured nine feet long and his stomach touched the ground.

MOST EXPENSIVE PIG
A Texas cross-bred Barrow sold for $56,000 in 1985.

BEST SURFER
A three-month-old pet pig named Chop Chop won the Wet Pet surfing contest in Hawaii in 1988. All kinds of animals were entered in the contest, but Chop Chop was the best. He rode the winning surfboard to victory with his proud owner, Brian Keaulana.

PIG FACTS

• Pigs range in height from 12 inches (miniature pigs) to four feet at the shoulder. Length (from the top of the head to the beginning of the tail) varies from about 20 inches to 6 feet. Adult pigs can weigh from 60 to 800 pounds.

• The lifespan of a pig ranges from 10 to 27 years.

• Sows usually give birth to a litter of six to 12 piglets. An average-sized newborn pig weighs from 2.5 to three pounds. To *farrow* means to give birth.

• A *hog* is a pig that is over three months old. A *gilt* is a female pig that has not had a litter. A *boar* is a male pig that is about six months old. A *runt* is the smallest pig in a litter.

• China has the largest hog population.

• There are 91 major domestic pig breeds throughout the world, subdivided into four types of breeds bred to produce various types of food: lard, bacon, and pork.

• During hot, humid weather, pigs like to cool off by wallowing (rolling over and over) in mud or dust.

• Pigs may eat their feed and leftovers like—well—*pigs,* but that doesn't mean they're stupid. In fact, pigs are among the most intelligent of all domestic animals.

Sheep

HIGHLIGHTS IN THE HISTORY OF SHEEP

• The wild ancestors of domesticated sheep lived in mountainous and plains areas all across the Northern Hemisphere. Today, wild sheep are found only in mountainous areas. One theory explaining their migration from the plains is that they retreated before an increasingly dominant animal—man.

• Sheep were among the first animals to be domesticated, more than 8,000 years ago.

• The earliest people to domesticate sheep probably lived in Western Asia.

• Sheep became an important source of energy food—high in protein and fat—for early humans. Because sheep were easy to handle and herd, primitive peoples were able to migrate from place to place with them.

• There is evidence that sheep wool was used in fabrics as early as 4000 B.C.

• Over the centuries, sheep have been bred for food, including milk. Their skins and fleeces have been used for a variety of purposes, including shoes and clothing.

SHEEP FACTS

• Like cattle and goats, sheep are ruminants (see "Cattle Facts," earlier in this chapter.) They eat grass, hay, silage (fodder such as cornstalks, hay, or straw, kept in a silo), legumes, weeds, herbs, and shrubs. Special feeds are manufactured for sheep ranchers to feed their animals.

• Some rams (male sheep) and ewes (females) have horns. The horns grow backward and downward, then curve forward in a spiral.

• A mature sheep can weigh from 60 to 400 pounds. The size of a sheep varies considerably, depending upon the breed.

• The lifespan of a sheep ranges from 12 to 20 years.

• Sheep's wool is usually white, but black, brown, or red wool is not uncommon.

• Newborn lambs can weigh from 4 to 18 pounds. Ram lambs are usually heavier than ewes. Most lambs are single births, but twins, triplets, and even quintuplets sometimes occur.

• Sheep are timid, nearly defenseless animals, easy prey for coyotes and other predators. They spend their time grazing and resting, follow their leader, and prefer to flock together.

• There are about 952 breeds of domestic sheep, classified into six types: fine, medium, long, and coarse-wool; crossbreeds; dairy; and fur and hair breeds.

• There are about one billion head of sheep in the world today. They are found worldwide, but the major sheep-raising countries are Australia, New Zealand, the Soviet Union, Argentina, India, South Africa, Turkey, the United States, Uruguay, Great Britain, Brazil, Iran, and Spain. Most American sheep ranches are located in the central and western parts of the country.

Creatures of the Sea

This chapter features an ocean of facts on fish and sea mammals: whales, dolphins, seals, sea lions, and walruses. You'll also find basic information on buying and caring for pet fish.

Creatures of the Sea

HISTORY

Fish are old animals—*very old*. The earliest known fish and the first vertebrate (an animal with a backbone) was the *Anatolepis,* which lived about 510 million years ago. Fossils of its scales have been found in the western United States.

The land-living vertebrates (mammals, reptiles, amphibians, and birds) evolved from fish.

PHYSICAL FACTS AND FISHY BEHAVIOR

• Fish breathe through **gills**, located in passages leading from the throat to the outside of the body. They breathe by taking water into their mouths, then forcing it out through the gill passages. As the water passes over the gills, oxygen moves into the gill capillaries (tiny tubes) and carbon dioxide pours out. A few fish have lungs as well as gills.

• Fish have muscular, **streamlined bodies.** They weave through the water and control their direction by using their fins. The scales, together with slimy secretions from its glands, form a nearly waterproof coating on a fish's body.

• Most fish are **cold-blooded,** which means they cannot regulate their body temperature, as mammals do. The body temperature of fish stays the same as that of their environment. But some species can stand water temperatures ranging from freezing to over 100°F.

• Many fish, especially those found in the tropics or subtropics, are **brightly colored.** Many also have body shapes or patterns that help to **camouflage** them when an enemy approaches.

• Fish can be **carnivorous** (eating other fish or organisms called plankton), **herbivorous** (eating underwater and floating plant life), or **omnivorous** (eating other fish, organisms, and plant life).

• Although most sharks give birth to live young, the majority of fish lay eggs, which are fertilized by the males after the females deposit them. Many species lay as many as five million eggs during one **spawn** (egg-laying process), because so many of the eggs remain unfertilized or are eaten by other animals.

• Many fish stay in tight groups called **schools.** Others are loners and congregate only for feeding and spawning.

NUMBER OF SPECIES

There are 30,000 species of fish. Of these, only 2,300 are freshwater fish.

WHERE TO FIND FISH

Fish are found in oceans, lakes, rivers, streams, and ponds all over the world, at all depths. Most stay in either salt or fresh water, but some species can adapt to both.

TOP FOUR SHARK FACTS

1. Unlike other species of fish, sharks don't have an organ called a swim bladder, which helps fish to breathe and to remain stable. Sharks are also heavyweights, so they have to keep moving, in order to breathe and stay upright in the water.

2. Sharks are found in all oceans, but the greatest number live in warm waters.

3. There are about 250 species of sharks. The shark most feared by humans is the great white shark, also known as the maneater. This shark can reach 20 feet in length and is probably responsible for more attacks than any other species. Other dangerous sharks are the tiger, blue, and mako. But the largest species, the whale and basking sharks, are harmless, easygoing fish that feed on plankton.

4. Sharks usually circle their prey before attacking and rarely swim near the surface of the water. If you see a fin cutting through the water, it's more likely to be the fin of a swordfish or dolphin than that of a shark. But it's always a good idea to be cautious when sharks are sighted. Swimmers should leave the water quickly and quietly, especially if they have a bleeding cut. Sharks are very sensitive to motion and to the smell of blood.

FIVE VENOMOUS SEA CREATURES

If you came across *any* of these creatures, get out of their way and out of the water fast! They sting and can sometimes cause paralysis or death.

Cone-shell

This is a small species of shellfish. Cone-shells feed on fish and worms, which they first paralyze with a poison contained in their teeth. The poison is also toxic to humans. Cone-shells are found in the South Pacific and the Indian Ocean.

Portuguese Man-of-War

This blue jellyfish is found on the ocean's surface in most warm-water regions. Its poisonous tentacles can extend up to 70 feet below the waterline.

Sea Wasps

The deadly poisonous tentacles of this jellyfish are up to 30 feet long. Sea wasps are found in the South Pacific.

Stingrays

This fish has broad, flat, winglike fins and a slender whiplike tail. The spines of its tail contain a painful, sometimes deadly poison. Stingrays are found in tropical and temperate seas.

Stonefish

This brownish-colored fish is the most venomous. It lies motionless at the bottom of shallow waters and can be mistaken for a rock. The spines of its fins contain a deadly poison. Stonefish are found in coral reefs of the South Pacific and the Indian Ocean.

FISH CHAMPS

HEAVIEST FRESHWATER FISH
The sturgeon
Weight: up to 2,250 lbs.

LARGEST FRESHWATER FISH
The rare Pa Beuk or Pla Buk, a giant catfish found in the Mekong
River of Laos and Thailand.
Length: 8 ft.
Weight: 360 lbs.

LARGEST SEA FISH
The whale shark
Length: up to 45 ft.
Weight: 12 tons (24,000 lbs.)

SMALLEST FISH
The dwarf goby, found in the Chagos Archipelago of the Indian
Ocean
Length: adult males, 0.338 in.; adult females, 0.350 in.

FASTEST FISH
The cosmopolitan sailfish
Speed: 68 mph, over a distance of 100 yards in three seconds

MOST ABUNDANT FISH
The three-inch-long bristlemouth, found in deep seas throughout
the world.

OLDEST FISH
Putte, a female European eel, who died in the aquarium of Sweden's Halsinborg Museum at the age of 88.

SHORTEST-LIVED FISH
The killifish of Africa and South America, which live for about
eight months in the wild.

OLDEST GOLDFISH
A goldfish named Fred died in Worthing, West Sussex, England,
in 1980 at the age of 41.

STRANGE BUT TRUE FACTS ABOUT FISH

• Flying fish glide through the air supported by air currents, and can stay aloft for a distance of 1,000 feet. These fish "fly" simply because they can, and enjoy doing it.

• Fish have been seen at depths of 35,000 feet. Since there is no light at such ocean depths, some of these fish are eyeless.

• The deadly piranha fish of South America swim and attack in schools of up to 1,000. They can strip an animal the size of a horse down to a skeleton in minutes and have been known to eat each other. They are considered a food delicacy by some people.

• The electric eel, a South American freshwater fish, can discharge from 450 to 650 volts of electricity—enough to light a neon bulb. They can perform this mysterious feat 40 times a second.

• Brazilian hiccup fish are so named because they swallow huge gulps of air and then release it, making a sound like a hiccup. The hiccup of a full-grown fish (12 feet) can be heard a mile away.

• Goby fish, found in tropical seas and rivers, have a dual respiratory system that lets them utilize oxygen from air as well as water. Thus they can survive on land.

• Remora fish use sharks for transportation. They attach themselves to a shark and are towed to a kill. There they detach themselves, feed, then reattach themselves to the shark.

FISH AS PETS

If you want a pet that won't answer back and doesn't have to be trained, one that's easy to take care of and fun to just sit back and watch, then fish are for you. Here is some basic information on buying and taking care of pet fish.

WHERE TO BUY FISH

The best place to buy pet fish is in a pet shop or a store that specializes in fish. Check the Yellow Pages for a shop in your city or town.

Five Tips on Choosing Fish

1. You'll probably want to choose freshwater fish. Saltwater fish and tanks can be very expensive to buy and maintain.

2. Decide how many fish you want. Fish usually range in price from a few dollars to as much as $150 for rare or exotic types like the African polka-dot catfish.

3. If you want more than one kind of fish, be sure to choose species that will get along with each other. Many are carnivorous and will eat other fish.

4. Make sure the fish are healthy. Check to see that no fins are missing, and that the fins aren't ragged. Check for fuzzy yellow or white spots on the body and pitted scales on the head. These could be signs of fungus or scale disease. Look at the eyes and the skin near the eyes to make sure there are no bulges or lumps. The eyes should be clear, not cloudy. Finally, you'll need to make sure the fish has a healthy appetite. Ask if you can give it some flake or pellet food, or try some worms or brine shrimp. Most fish in a shop aren't fed as much as pet fish, so they should snap up the food you give them. A good appetite is a sign of health.

5. Ask your salesperson for help in choosing fish.

The Aquarium

The kind of aquarium you get depends on how many fish you're buying, how much room you have for a tank, and how much money you want to spend. A medium-sized tank holding about 20 gallons of water is good for two or three fish. Also, some experts recommend buying long, low tanks rather than narrow, deep ones. This is because oxygen is distributed better in the longer tank. You'll also need an air pump for oxygenating the water in the tank and a filter for keeping the water clean. Ask the salesperson for advice on tanks, pumps, and filters. Also ask if the water in your tank needs to be heated, purified, and/or softened. Aquarium gravel should be placed at the bottom of the tank to allow fish waste and uneaten food to be totally decomposed by the bacteria that live in the gravel. And fish need light, so make sure your aquarium includes a fluorescent fixture.

Bringing Your Fish Home

Your fish will be in a water-filled bag when you buy it. It's important to handle the bag gently and carefully. Your tank should be set up and waiting. When you get home, gently place the bag in the water and let it float in the tank for half an hour. This will give your fish a chance to get used to the temperature of the water. After half an hour, take the bag out of the tank and cut it open. Then pour the water through a net into the sink, allowing the fish to tumble gently into the fishnet. Pet shop water should never mix with the water in your tank; it's too dirty. Also, never touch a fish with you hands. Touching a fish will disturb the layer of slime on its body that protects its scales. Carry the fish to the tank right away and ease it in.

Feeding Your Fish

Fish eat commercially prepared food, including frozen, freeze-dried, and pellet foods. Feed your fish small amounts of food several times a day. Most adult fish can be fed in the mornings and evenings. Live food such as earthworms or brine shrimp are treats your pet fish might enjoy about once a week.

Ten Species of Pet Fish

Goldfish

Mollies

Jewel Cichlid

Rusty Cichlid

Oscar

Malawian Eye Eater

Malawian Auratus

Albino Channel Catfish

Golden Ram

Black-bellied Upside-down Catfish

For more information on caring for pet fish, check your local library for books on the subject.

Sea Mammals

WHALES

HISTORY

Whales originated about 70 million years ago in the early Tertiary or Upper Cretaceous period. They split off from a group of land-dwelling carnivorous mammals.

FAMILY AND TYPES

Whales are also known as *Cetaceans,* because they belong to a family of marine (ocean) mammals called *Cetacea.* Smaller members of this family are dolphins and porpoises.

Cetaceans are divided into three types:

Archaeoceti—A group of toothed whales, now extinct.

Odontoceti—About 70 species of modern toothed whales, including sperm whales (the most numerous species), killer, beluga, and beaked whales, and dolphins and porpoises.

Mysticeti—Thirteen species of toothless baleen (whalebone) whales. Baleen include the blue whale (the largest whale), the minke (the smallest), humpbacks, right or bowhead whales, and gray whales.

WHERE FOUND

• Cetaceans are found in oceans throughout the world. They also inhabit some tropical lakes.

PHYSICAL FACTS, FEATS, AND BEHAVIOR

• Although they're warm-blooded vertebrates, whales are adapted for sea life by having fishlike bodies, nearly hairless skin, and an insulation layer of blubber, which can be up to 12 inches thick.

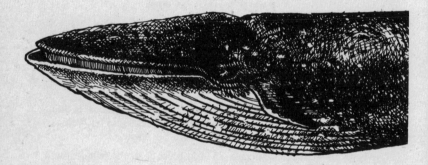

• Whales also have front flippers and flat tails that propel them through the water. They have lungs and blow holes on top of their heads for breathing in and out.

• Average-sized adult whales of various species range from 4 to 100 feet long and weigh from 45 pounds to 220 tons. (The largest dinosaur, *Brachiosaurus,* weighed less than *half* as much as a female blue whale.)

• A whale's lifespan is from 20 to 70 years. Except for humans, the only predator of large whales is the killer whale.

• Baleen whales eat different kinds of plankton. Their mouths have a sievelike structure for straining plankton from the water.

Odontoceti are carnivores. They eat fish, squid, and octopus, seizing prey with their teeth and swallowing it whole.

• Most baleen whales migrate twice a year between rich feeding areas in the Arctic and Antarctic to temperate or subtropical breeding and calving sites.

• Baleen whales are usually solitary; Odontoceti live in schools ranging from a few whales to 1,000 or more.

• A baby whale (calf) is born underwater. After birth, the mother whale pushes her calf to the water's surface for its first breath.

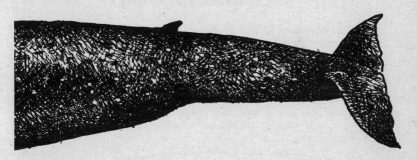

• Whales are good high-jumpers. They often leap 20 feet or more into the air.

• Whales that live in polar waters face the danger of becoming trapped in the ice and starving or suffocating. In October, 1988, three gray whales became trapped in Barrow, Alaska. The U.S. and the U.S.S.R. mounted a joint rescue operation to free the whales. One of the whales died, but two were saved when Soviet ice-breakers plowed through the ice so the whales could reach the open sea for their migration to warmer waters.

• Whales sometimes become beached (stranded). These whales are usually outgoing species like sperm or pilot whales, or dolphins. Many of these strandings may result from navigational errors—the whales get lost and swim into waters too shallow for them. A single stranded whale or dolphin is almost always sick.

WHALE TALK

Whales make a variety of sounds. Baleen whales make low-pitched moans; short gruntlike thumps and knocks; chirps, cries, and whistles; and clicks, or "pulses." The origin of these sounds may be the larynx, although whales have no vocal cords. Humpback whales make a moaning, "singing" sound, which has been recorded and can be heard on records and tapes.

Odontoceti make clicking and whistling sounds that may come from either the larynx or nasal passages.

THE ENDANGERED WHALE

Whales have been hunted for oil and meat since the 1600s, possibly earlier. But overhunting has decreased whale populations and endangered some species. Below is the current population status of five different types of whales:

BLUE WHALE   Reduced from a population of about 200,000 in the early 1900s to about 5,000 today.

HUMPBACKS   All populations have been greatly reduced in the 20th century. However, commercial hunting of humpbacks has been prohibited since 1966.

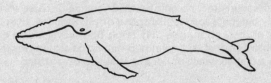

BOWHEAD OR RIGHT WHALES

Among the first whales to be hunted commercially, these animals were severly reduced in numbers during the 1800s. A few populations in the Southern Hemisphere seem to be increasing, but the world population is probably less than 5,000. This is considered to be the most endangered species of baleen whale.

GRAY WHALE

Now extinct in the North Atlantic. There are only a few hundred gray whales in the western Pacific, but the California gray whale population has increased to about 20,000, as of 1988. They are protected from commercial whaling, but about 180 are caught by Soviet whalers each year.

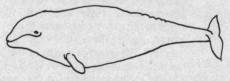

SPERM WHALE

Once heavily hunted for ambergris, a waxy substance used as a base for perfumes and cosmetics. Factory-ship whaling of this species was prohibited in 1979. Female sperm whales are numerous, but the male population has been greatly reduced.

TOP 10 DOLPHIN FACTS

• There are more than 50 species of dolphins. The best-known and best-loved species are the common and the bottlenosed:

COMMON DOLPHIN These dolphins are black or brown on the back, with lighter stripes on the sides and a white belly. The average length of the common dolphin is eight feet, average weight, 165 pounds. They are often sighted playing around the bows of fishing boats. They travel with schools of tuna and have been known to lead the schools to escape from nets. Large numbers of dolphins are killed annually when they get caught in the nets. They are found worldwide.

BOTTLE-NOSED DOLPHIN These are the lovable stars of aquarium and marine shows. They are black or slate blue, with a lighter-colored belly and dark flippers. The shape of the snout, together with the curve of the mouth, give these dolphins an appealing "smile." The average length of the bottlenosed is nine feet; the average weight is 350 pounds. They're trained to do acrobatics such as jumping through flamed hoops, leaping in pairs (sometimes as high as 30 feet in the air), and other circuslike routines. Bottlenosed are found in the coastal waters of the North Atlantic and in the Mediterranean Sea.

• The lifespan of dolphins is about 25 to 35 years in the wild, less in captivity. Dolphins who are unhappy in captivity will commit suicide by starvation, batter their heads against walls, or drown themselves.

• Dolphins sleep at night, just below the surface of the water. They rise for air about every three or four minutes.

• Dolphins eat small fish, crustaceans (shrimp, lobtser, crab), squid, herring, and sardines. They can dive to depths of 70 feet and stay underwater for 15 minutes.

• Dolphins sometimes swim alone or in pairs, but they usually congregate in large herds, often numbering in the hundreds.

• Dolphins can reach speeds of 30 miles per hour, but their usual speed is 20 to 24 miles per hour.

• Like other whales, dolphins have their own special "language." They communicate with each other by using a wide range of underwater sounds, or pulses. Dolphin noises include clicks and whistles. Researchers aided by computers have tried to learn the dolphin language and to teach dolphins human speech, either by word or translated into whistles.

• Dolphins are intelligent, playful animals. They are capable of imitation, memorization, and learning by observation. They can communicate their experience, solve complicated problems, and perform complex tasks. Dolphins don't respond to training only because they want to please humans—they do it because it's fun.

• Dolphins are often mistaken for porpoises, and vice versa. But dolphins are generally larger than porpoises. Dolphins also have long, beaklike snouts, while porpoises have blunt snouts.

• There are recorded accounts of dolphins leading fishing boats to rescue a trapped dolphin or piloting lost fishermen out of fogs. In one incident, three dolphins saved a woman who had fallen off a boat in the Indian Ocean. One dolphin buoyed her up, while the others circled her, probably to keep her safe from sharks. Eventually, they all drifted toward a marker in the sea. The woman clung to the marker until she was spotted by a rescue ship. She had traveled 200 miles, and the dolphins stayed with her the entire time.

SEALS, SEA LIONS, AND WALRUSES

- These sea mammals are also called *pinnipeds*. Pinnipeds are aquatic mammals whose four limbs have been modified into flippers.

- Pinnipeds have streamlined bodies that are rounded in the middle and tapered at the ends. They all have a thick layer of fat beneath the skin.

- Nearly all pinnipeds live in oceans and most inhabit cold or temperate regions. Some live most of the year in open ocean; others live in coastal waters and spend time on shore or on ice floes. They give birth on land and spend several months there nursing their pups.

- Most pinnipeds eat fish and shellfish. Many are able to dive deep into the water to find food. Sea lions have been known to dive as deep as 600 feet for food.

- Pinnipeds have a keen sense of hearing and echolocation (sonar) for underwater navigation.

SEALS AND SEA LIONS

- Fur seals and sea lions belong to the same animal family. Both have ears outside their bodies. A second type of seal, the true or earless seal, has a pair of inner ears.

- True seals and sea lions have short, coarse hair. Fur seals have an outer coat of long coarse hair and an inner coat of thick, soft fur.

- Sea lions, fur seals, and walruses can turn their hind flippers forward for walking on land. They swim by moving their long front flippers in a rowing motion. True seals can't rotate their hind flippers—they wriggle on their bellies and pull themselves forward with their short front flippers. They swim in a side-to-side motion with sweeping movements of their hind flippers.

- The performing seals seen in circuses and on TV are actually sea lions.

• Sea lions were once hunted for their blubber and hides, but today there is very little hunting of sea lions.

Three Species of True Seals

ELEPHANT SEAL

The largest pinniped, reaching lengths of 18 feet, and weighing up to 5,000 pounds (males). The northern elephant seal of California was hunted almost to extinction in the 1800s. Now there is a colony in the Santa Barbara Islands, off the coast of California. The southern species lives in the southern seas and in waters close to Antarctica.

HARBOR SEAL

Found along coasts and in sheltered bays and harbors of North America, Europe, and Northeast Asia. It's the most commonly seen seal. Some are found in rivers and in the Great Lakes. Harbor seals are about six feet long and weigh up to 250 pounds. Their coats are gray with white spots, or yellowish with gray or black blotches.

HARP SEALS

Found in the North Atlantic around Greenland. In the summer, they migrate south to the Newfoundland and Norwegian coasts, where they breed in large groups. Pups are born on ice floes and are covered with fluffy white fur. They have long been hunted and killed ruthlessly for their fur, but animal activist groups are trying to stop the killing. Hunting of baby harp seals has been regulated, but not stopped.

Two Species of Sea Lions

CALIFORNIA SEA LION
The dark-brown, playful circus "seals." This species is found in waters off the coast of California. Males grow up to eight feet long and weigh up to 500 pounds.

NORTHERN OR STELLAR'S SEA LION
One of the largest pinnipeds. Males grow up to 13 feet long and weigh up to 1,800 pounds. This species of sea lion is found in the Bering Sea, near the Aleutian Islands, and along the Pacific coast from northern Japan to southern California.

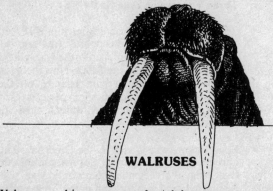

WALRUSES

Walruses are big sea mammals. Adult males are up to 10 ft. long and weigh up to 3,000 lbs. Their tusks can grow to three ft. and weigh over 10 lbs.

• Walruses aren't strong swimmers, but they sometimes dive as deep as 240 ft. for food. They eat mostly shellfish, especially mollusks.

• Walruses use their tusks for prying shellfish from the ocean floor and for pulling themselves up onto ice floes.

• These pinnipeds live in shallow water and spend most of their time on ice floes and beaches in herds of about 100 animals. The herds follow the ice line, moving south in winter and north in summer.

• The walrus is important to the Eskimos, who hunt it for food and clothing. Walrus hunting since the 1600s has greatly reduced the population. Several nations now have laws regulating walrus hunting.

• There are two types of walruses—Atlantic and Pacific. The Atlantic walrus was once found as far south as Nova Scotia and Massachusetts. It is now an endangered species.

SEA MAMMAL CHAMPS

LARGEST AND HEAVIEST
The blue whale (also the world's largest and heaviest mammal)
Length: 100 ft.
Weight: 150 tons (300,000 lbs.)

LIGHTEST WEIGHT
Commerson's dolphin, found in waters off the southern tip of South America
Weight: 50.7 to 77.1 lbs.

LARGEST PINNIPED
Southern elephant seal
Length: 16½ ft. (males)
Weight: 5,000 lbs.

SMALLEST PINNIPEDS
The ringed seal of the Arctic, the Baikal seal of Lake Baikal in the U.S.S.R., and the Caspian seal of the U.S.S.R.'s Caspian Sea.
Length: 5 ft., 6 in. (male)
Weight: 280 lbs. (male). Females are about ⅔ this size.

FASTEST PINNIPED
California sea lion
Speed: 25 mph

DEEPEST-DIVING PINNIPED
Female northern elephant seal, off the coast of California in 1983.
Depth: 2,067 ft.

HIGHEST-PRICED SEA CREATURES
Orky and Corky, a pair of killer whales exhibited at Marineland of the Pacific in Palos Verdes, California. They are the world's only captive breeding pair of killer whales. In 1985 Orky and Corky were worth $2 million.

Birds

Here are facts on fine-feathered birds in your own backyard, around your house, and around the world, plus the biggest, smallest, fastest, most talkative, and strangest birds on earth.

History

Birds evolved about 140 million years ago from the *Archaeopteryx*, a small, flying reptilelike creature that had a tail, feathers, clawed wings, and jaws with teeth.

About 70 million years ago, there were 1.5 million bird species; today there about 9,000 species. Most species became extinct through the natural process of evolution (they couldn't adapt to changes in their environment); a few species, including the dodo, the passenger pigeon, the Carolina parakeet, and the heath hen have been destroyed by humans.

Experts think that all the bird species found today existed in their present form by the Pleistocene era (1 million to 8150 B.C.).

Physical Facts About Birds

• Birds are warm-blooded, egg-laying vertebrates. Their body temperature is about 2° to 14°F. higher than that of mammals.

• Birds have keen eyesight and hearing, but very little sense of smell.

• The majority of birds are highly adapted for flying. Their bodies are light, strong, and compact. Their muscles, bones, and organs are coordinated so as to maintain balance in flight.

• Some birds are unable to fly, including the cassowary, the flightless cormorant, emu, kiwi, ostrich, penguin, rail, rhea, and domestic chicken. Their bodies are simply not adapted for flying.

• The feathers of birds are very light in weight, but they are excellent protectors against cold and moisture. Many birds lose their feathers in the late summer, then grow new ones a short time later. This annual process, called *molting,* is gradual, as birds cannot fly without their feathers. Some birds molt again in the spring, changing from dull to bright plumage for the mating season. Young birds may molt three times during their first year, from baby down to adult plumage.

• Birds can be herbivorous, carnivorous, or omnivorous, depending on the species and its habitat. Non-meat-eating birds will feed on fruit, grains, plants, flower nectar, wild rice, seeds, and grasses. Carnivorous birds may eat small mammals, fish, crabs, shellfish, insects, spiders, reptiles, amphibians, carrion, other birds, and, of course, worms.

Bird Songs and Bird Talk

• As everyone knows, a lot of birds make musical trilling sounds. These sounds, called *birdsong,* are classified into types: flight song, feeding, nest, flock, aggressive, alarm, and defense of territory. Birdsong is usually produced by males and reaches its peak during the breeding season. The best bird singers include the bobolink, southern mockingbird, hermit and wood thrushes, purple and house finches, canyon wren, and the European skylark and nightingale.

• Most birds have favorite singing spots, including fence posts, treetops, thickets, the forest floor, or in the air, as they fly.

• Many birds are good mimics. They can imitate other birds' voices or the voices of humans. Wild bird mimics include mimic thrushes, jays, crows, and starlings. Some birds that develop their imitative powers in captivity are canaries, finches, parrots, ravens, crows, and mynahs.

Migration

• In the spring and fall, flocks of birds migrate, which means they move from one region to another (usually north-south in fall and the reverse in the spring) for feeding, and nesting. Some birds travel hundreds or even thousands of miles during their migrations.

• Birds that migrate at night often navigate by the stars; however, they sometimes get lost in heavy fog. Day-migrating birds navigate by the sun and keep their eyes on the shoreline.

• In North America, the north-south migration routes birds use are known as *flyways*. The four major flyways are the Pacific, central, Mississippi, and Atlantic. The space inside a flyway used by a particular group of birds is called a *corridor*.

• Not all birds migrate in a north-south direction. Many European birds go west to the mild climate of the British Isles, then back east in the spring. Mountain-dwelling birds migrate to lower altitudes in winter.

• The Arctic tern makes the longest migration of any bird—from the Arctic to the Antarctic and back again (22,000 miles). Artic terns leave the Arctic in August and return from Antarctica by mid-June. It breeds during the Arctic summer when there is constant daylight, then heads for the Antarctic to spend another summer of constant daylight in the Southern Hemisphere.

Birds' Nests

• Most birds build a nest in which to lay their eggs. Some birds weave complicated nests of twigs, grass, leaves, and sometimes pieces of cloth or string. Other birds lay their eggs on a few twigs or on the ground.

• Most sea birds, shore birds, and game birds lay their eggs on rocky ledges or in shallow holes in the sand or ground. Ducks and geese make nests out of weeds and grasses and line them with their feathers (called *down*).

• Woodpeckers and parrots make their nests in hollow trees. Storks' nests are platforms made of sticks. Eagles' nests, called *aeries,* are built at the tops of trees or on mountainsides.

Bird-Brained Facts
(Strange But True)

Plovers (wading birds) of Egypt ride on the backs of crocodiles. They enter the crocodile's mouth to pick food from between its teeth.

Bee hummingbirds are incredibly tiny. Eighteen of them weigh only one ounce.

A type of South America bird, the **hoatzin,** is born with claws on its wings as well as on its feet. These wing claws allow the hoatzin to climb around in trees.

Red-eyed vireos are very musical—in fact, they have perfect pitch. They will repeat their calls, note for note, 22,000 times a day without going flat or sharp.

Hummingbirds have the amazing ability to hover in midair, like a helicopter, and to fly backward.

Birds take dust baths. They put dust on their feathers and then shake and preen it off. They do this to get rid of parasites like lice and mites that crawl in and between their feathers. The roughness of the dust helps to loosen the parasites.

South Africa weaver birds lay their eggs in communal nests. The nests contain 100 or more separate apartments for the bird families.

South American tiger birds are so named because they can imitate a tiger's voice.

Unlike most birds, **mound-builder birds** of Australia have all their feathers when they're hatched and can fly right after birth.

Ostriches, the world's largest nonflying birds, can kick like a mule, imitate a lion's voice, and hiss like a snake.

Ostrich babies that are hatched first are fed the unhatched ostrich eggs.

Storks stand for long periods of time on one leg. They can do this because their joints are self-locking.

The **three-wattled bell bird** of Costa Rica has a call that can be heard for three miles.

The Birds of North America

Listed below are facts on some of the best-known birds seen in the United States and parts of Canada. The measurements given refer to body length unless otherwise noted.

Bird	Types	Facts & Features
Blackbird	Brewer's, Rusty	The Brewer's is often seen on western ranches and perched on corrals.
Bluebird	Eastern, Western, Mountain	Bluebirds aren't totally blue—their breasts are either brown or white.
Blue Jay	Eastern, Stellar's, Pinyon, Scrub	Noisy blue jays have a blue back and tail. The Eastern, Stellar's, and Scrub have crests on their heads.
Bobolink	—	Bobolinks have a light-colored back and a black head and chest. Their song is one of the most beautiful.
Bobwhite	Scaled, Gambel's, California, Mountain	Often called quails or partridges, bobwhites have brown bodies and short, stout bills. Their name comes from their call, "bob-white." The young can often be seen walking in a row behind their mother.
Bunting	Indigo, Blue Grosbeak, Lazuli, Painted	Buntings are totally blue in color.

Bird	Types	Facts & Features
Cardinal	Northern, *Pyrrhuloxia*	The Northern has a red body; the *Pyrrhuloxia* is gray, with a red face, crest, breast, and tail.
Catbird	—	The catbird is slate-gray with a black cap. Its name comes from its mewing call.
Chickadee	Black-capped, Brown-capped, Chestnut-capped	The call of this plump, buff-colored bird is what gives it its name.
Crow	American, Fish, Common Raven	An often seen all black bird. The fish crow's loud call sounds like "Car, car!"

Bird	Types	Facts & Features
Cuckoo	Yellow-billed, Black-billed	These are long, slim birds with slightly curved bills. Cuckoos are among the few birds that eat hairy caterpillars.
Dove	Rock (Domestic Pigeon), Mourning	Chunky, broad-tailed rock doves are the well-known city-dwelling pigeons. Mourning doves are slimmer, with brown bodies and long tails.
Duck	Mallard, American Black, Wood, Northern Pintail, Canvasback, Common Merganser	These are swimming birds that can also walk well on their large webbed feet. Canvasbacks and mergansers are good divers.

Bird	Types	Facts & Features
Eagle	Bald, Golden	The eagles are large (32 inches long) soaring birds. The bald eagle, the national emblem, is usually found near water and its favorite food—fish. It takes several years for bald eaglets to get their adult plumage.
Falcon	Peregrine, American Kestrel, Merlin	Among the falcons, the reddish-brown Kestrel is the smallest (8½ inches long); the dark-colored Merlin is 12 inches long; the 15-inch long Peregrine is a rare blue or brown-backed species that nests on cliffs and some tall buildings.
Finch	Purple, House	The brown house finch is often seen in suburban areas.
Goldfinch	American	This bird has a yellow body, black cap and wings, and a swooping flight pattern like that of a roller coaster.
Goose	Canada	These are large swimming birds with long black necks. They fly in a *V* formation and feed in ponds and estuaries. They also eat weeds, grass, and grains.
Gull	Herring	These light-colored marine birds are often seen on the Atlantic coast and flying around landfills. They are scavengers, eating carrion and garbage; they also eat small fish, shellfish, insects, and blueberries.

Hawk	Cooper's, Northern, Goshawk, Red-tailed	Hawks have sharply hooked bills, powerful feet with curved talons, and broad, rounded wings. They are graceful fliers and have keen eyesight. The large (18 inches long) brown-backed Red-Tailed is a soaring hawk.
Heron	Great Blue	A large (38 inches), long-legged wading bird. Its call is a series of low-pitched croaks.
Hummingbird	Ruby-throated	This tiny (3 inches long) brightly colored bird lives in the eastern United States. It can hover in midair without moving and fly backward. It eats insects and the nectar of flowers.
Kingfisher	Belted	This bird has a grayish-green back, a ragged crest, and a long beak. It dives headfirst into water to catch fish. It has a harsh, rattling call.

Bird	Types	Facts & Features
Loon	Common	A large, long-bodied swimming and deep-diving bird. Loons kick along the water before taking flight.
Magpie	Black-billed, Yellow-billed	This black and white long-tailed bird is a relative of the crow. It flies and feeds in flocks and is often seen around ranches.
Meadowlark	Horned Lark, Eurasian Skylark	Brown-and-yellow horned larks feed in flocks in fields and along shores, walking as they feed. They eat insects, seeds, and grasses.
Mockingbird	Northern	This grayish bird nests around homes and perches on chimneys and TV antennas. It imitates other birds' songs perfectly, but adds notes of its own.
Oriole	Northern (Baltimore), Orchard	The black or dark-green-and-orange Baltimore oriole hangs its nest from the end of a branch on shade or fruit trees.
Osprey	Also called the Fish Hawk	Brown-and-white ospreys soar over lakes, bays, and oceans catching fish with their feet. They make their large nests in trees, on towers, and on man-made structures near water.

Bird	Types	Facts & Features
Owl	Common Barn, Great Horned, Eastern and Western Screech	The barn owl has a white, heart-shaped face, dark eyes, buff-collored body, and long legs. It nests in barns, church belfries, and hollow trees and has a hissing call. The great horned owl is a large brown bird with ear tufts. Its call is a series of five to seven deep hoots, all on the same pitch. Screech Owls are gray or brown, have keen eyesight, and whistle rather than screech, despite their name.
Pheasant	Ring-necked	A brightly colored (males only), long-tailed game bird that scratches the ground for food, including grain. The hen pheasant is smaller, and brown and white in color.
Robin	American, also known as the Red Breast	Robins nest in every Canadian province and U.S. state except Hawaii. Their eggs are light blue.
Sandpiper	Lesser Yellow-legs, Spotted, Least	These are small-bodied (4 to 8 inches long) long-legged shore or marsh birds.
Sparrow	House (also called the English Sparrow), Junco	The house sparrow is probably the best known type. It was imported from England in 1850. House sparrows are often found in cities, and they nest in buildings and bird houses.

Bird	Types	Facts & Features
Swallow	Tree, Barn	The tree swallow is blue-black and white; the barn swallow is chestnut and buff-colored and has a deeply forked "swallow tail." It nests in barns and under bridges.
Swan	Tundra (Whistling), Mute	The tundra is a very large (36 inches long) all-white black-beaked bird that migrates in flocks in a *V* formation from the Arctic to the coastal United States. It uses its long neck to reach underwater vegetation. The orange-beaked mute swan is found in the Great Lakes, coastal waters, and city parks.
Thrush	Wood, Hermit	Both types have brown backs and spotted breasts. The wood thrush has a clear, flutelike song.
Vulture	Turkey, Black	Large (22 - 25 inches long) scavenger birds that soar for miles on air currents. Turkey vultures have bald red heads; black vultures have bald black heads.
Whippoorwill	—	This brown night bird is usually heard but not seen, since it rarely flies by day. Its call gives it its name.
Woodpecker	Red-headed	This red-headed bird is often seen on tree trunks, where it uses its bill to peck out insects.
Wren	House	Small (4½ inches long) brown birds often found in gardens and parks. They nest in hollow trees and bird houses.

Birds of Other Continents and Countries

(Measurements refer to body lengths unless otherwise noted)

Bird	Where Found	Facts & Features
Canary	The Canary Islands, Azores, Madiera Island, Africa, Europe	Members of the finch family, wild canaries have olive-green backs and yellow breasts.
Cockatoo	Australia, New Guinea (Black Cockatoos)	This white or pink bird has a short, blunt tail, a long bill, and a yellow or red crest. The black cockatoo has dark plumage.
Emu	Australia	There is only one species of this tall (5 to 6 feet) flightless bird. Emus resemble ostriches. They are swift runners and are easily tamed.

Bird	Where Found	Facts & Features
Flamingo	Africa, Asia, Europe, West Indies, South America, Galápagos Islands, Florida (rarely seen)	This tall (5 to 6½ feet) pink or red wading bird scoops its large saw-like bill through the water to strain out its food—plants, shellfish, and frogs. Its nest is a one-to-two-foot high cone of mud with a hole in the center.

Bird	Where Found	Facts & Features
Myna or Mynah	Southeastern Asia, especially India and Sri Lanka	The best known is the Hill Mynah, a large (12 to 15 inches long) black bird whose calls range from low chuckles to loud whistles. They can be trained to talk and are better mimics than parrots.
Ostrich	Africa, Southwest Asia	The largest nonflying bird (7 - 8 feet tall). The male ostrich is black, the female, grayish-brown. Only the male has long white plumes. The ostrich can run at speeds up to 50 mph and kicks powerfully to defend itself.
Parakeet	Asia, from India to Malaysia; Australia	A small parrot. The best known is the shell, or *budgerigar,* of Australia. "Budgies" come in a variety of colors and are popular pets. (The word *budgerigar* means "pretty good" in the language of the Australian Bushmen.)
Parrot	Africa, Central and South America, New Zealand, New Guinea	There are 315 species of parrots, including various types of parakeets, macaws, lovebirds, and cockatoos. Parrots are brightly colored, with large heads, short necks, strong feet, and a strong, hooked bill. They live in tropical forests and eat seeds and fruit. They are popular as pets. The African gray parrot is the best mimic.

Bird	*Where Found*	*Facts & Features*
Peacock	Africa, Asia	Peacocks are members of the pheasant family. The males have bright blue or green feathers and huge tails that fan out to show eyelike colorful spots. Peacocks roost in trees. They are solitary birds that like to be left alone.

Pelican	North and South America	White or brown lake and sea bird. The American white pelican is 5 feet tall and has a 10-foot wingspread. Pelicans store fish in pouches below their bills. The young feed from the pouch and throat.

Bird	*Where Found*	*Facts & Features*
Penguin	Antarctica, Australia, New Zealand	Flightless black- or blue-and-white swimming and diving birds that waddle on land and sometimes slide on their bellies on the ice. They use their flipperlike wings to swim and their webbed feet as rudders. The largest are the emperor and king penguins (3 to 4 feet tall).
Stork	Africa, Asia, Europe, Mexico to Argentina, U.S.	White and black long-legged diving birds, storks have no voice boxes and are mute. They communicate by clattering their bills. In Europe the white stork is thought to bring good luck. The American wood stork is the only stork that nests in the United States.

Toucan

	From Mexico to Argentina, ranging from sea level to 10,000 feet in the Andes Mountains	Tree-roosting toucans vary in size from the jay-sized toucanet to the 24 inches long toco toucan of the Amazon. The toco is black-and-white with a long orange bill. The toucan's chief food is fruits and berries. It also steals other birds' young and eggs.

Bird Champs

**(Birds definitely win the award for most champs
in the animal kingdom.)**

Heaviest Bird of Prey

The Andean condor
  Weight: 20 - 25 lbs.

Largest and Heaviest Nonflying Birds

The North African ostrich
  Height: 9 ft.
  Weight: 345 lbs.

Heaviest Flying Bird

The kori bustard of East and
South Africa
  Weight: 40 lbs.

Fastest-Flying Birds

The peregrine falcon
  Speed: 217 mph
The white-throated spinetail
swift
  Speed: 105.6 mph

Lightest Bird of Prey

The white-fronted falconet of
Borneo
  Weight: 1.23 oz.

Smallest and Lightest Sea Bird

The least storm (or stormy) pe-
trel of Mexico
  Length: 5.5. in.
  Weight: About 1 oz.

Smallest and Lightest Bird

The bee hummingbird of Cuba
and The Isle of Pines
  Length: 2.24 in.
  Weight: 0.056 oz.

Highest-Flying Birds

In 1967, 30 whooping swans
were spotted flying at 27,000
feet. However, this record is
topped by geese, who often fly
over Mt. Everest in the Asian
Himalayas at a height of
30,000 feet.

Smallest Bird Eggs

The eggs of two Jamaican Vervain hummingbirds.
Length: Less than 0.39 in.
Weight: 0.0128 oz and 0.0132 oz.

Chattiest Bird

Prudie, a male African gray parrot that has a vocabulary of about 1,000 words. Prudie has won the "best talking parrot-like bird" title at the National Cage and Aviary Bird Show in London for 12 years in a row.

Rarest Bird

A dusky seaside sparrow living at Discovery Island, Disney World. It is the last bird of its species. The next rarest bird is probably the California condor. Scientists have been trying to save the species by breeding a pair of condors in captivity.

Longest-Airborne Bird

The sooty tern, which stays in the air, continuously awake, for three to four years after breeding. After that time, it returns to the breeding grounds.

Oldest Bird

A male great sulphur-crested cockatoo at the London Zoo was over 80 years old when he died in 1982.

Birds with the Keenest Eyesight

Birds of prey such as eagles, hawks, and falcons have eyesight that is about eight to 10 times stronger than human vision. Golden eagles can spot a hare from two miles away. Peregrine falcons can spot a pigeon from five miles away.

Deepest Diver

The emperor penguin of the Antarctic can dive to a depth of 870 feet and sometimes stays underwater for 18 minutes.

Biggest Bird Nest

In 1963 a pair of bald eagles in Florida built a nest that was 9½ feet wide and 20 feet deep; it weighed more than 6,700 lbs.

Biggest Bird Eggs

Ostrich eggs
Length: 6 - 8 in.
Diameter: 4 - 6 in.
Weight: 3.63 - 3.88 lbs.

Birds as Pets

Birds can be fine feathered friends—amusing, lively, lovable, and fairly easy to care for. Below are some basics on choosing, housing, and taking care of pet birds.

CHOOSING YOUR BIRD

After you and your family decide that a bird will fit into your household, you'll need to decide what kind of bird you want. The most popular kinds of small pet birds are budgies (the most popular), other types of parakeets, canaries, and finches. Your choice will depend partly on how much you want to spend. Birds range in price from several dollars to several hundred dollars. The rarer or more exotic birds like parrots, mynahs, toucans, or cockatoos are more expensive than the smaller birds. It's a good idea to check out more than one pet store to compare prices.

Before you buy your bird, you'll need to make sure it is healthy. A healthy bird eats, is active, and is alert to its surroundings. Some birds, such as doves or parrots, normally sit still. However, a bird that sits in a corner or on the floor may be sick. A bird that has dirty vent feathers (the bottom feathers just above the tail) is definitely sick. All the feathers should be sleek and smooth.

CAGES

Once you've picked out the perfect pet bird, you'll need to buy it a cage to live in. The cage should be big enough for your bird to spread and flap its wings. Your bird should also be able to fly comfortably from one side of the cage to the other, or up and down (little finches like to fly vertically). The paint on the cage should be nontoxic and lead-free.

Your bird's cage should contain:

Seed and water cups that are easy to fill and clean.

Perches that fit your bird's feet and that are spaced evenly throughout the cage. One perch should be directly in front of (not over) the feeding cups.

A pull-out tray at the bottom for bird droppings. This kind of tray is used so that the cage can be cleaned without disturbing your bird. You can also use newspaper to cover the bottom, but some experts feel that the newsprint can be poisonous to birds. Precut or graveled bird-cage paper is another alternative.

FOOD AND TOYS

Ask your pet-store salesperson which kind of prepared or natural foods (like seeds) are best for your bird. A cuttlebone (the shell of a cuttlefish) will supply your bird with minerals it needs and will keep its beak trimmed. You'll need some gravel as well, since seed-eating birds have no teeth and need gravel to help them digest their food.

Ask about toys your bird might enjoy playing with, such as bells, mirrors, and climbing apparatus.

AFTER YOU BRING YOUR BIRD HOME

The best place to hang your bird's cage is somewhere shady and away from drafts. Cats and dogs should be kept away from your bird and its cage; it's a good idea to hang the cage out of reach of other pets. Younger kids also need to be taught to respect your new pet—they should talk softly to the bird and should never stick their fingers in the cage. Your bird may feel free to take a nip at curious fingers.

FIVE BASICS OF BIRD CARE

1. Give your bird fresh water in its cup every day. Add fresh food when the food cup is getting low.

2. Make sure your bird has a fresh supply of gravel and a new cuttlebone when needed.

3. The cage should be washed and disinfected every month. The perches should be scraped and the paper on the bottom of the cage changed at least once a week.

4. Many people like to cover their bird's cage at night. This can be a good idea in cold weather, because the covering will help to keep in the heat. Covering your bird's cage isn't necessary in warm weather.

5. Call your vet immediately if your bird seems sick or unresponsive.

SAFETY TIPS

If your bird is trained to take some flights around the house, you'll need to watch it closely. Keep your bird out of the kitchen and away from other pets, fans, fireplaces, and open windows. Some people clip their birds' wings to keep them from flying away. This is *not* a good idea. Without wings, your bird cannot protect itself and can even get stepped on if it is on the floor (it won't be able to get out of the way quickly). In general, it's best to keep your bird in its cage. With love and the proper care, your bird will be a happy, healthy caged pet.

Rodents

As you probably know, squirrels, rats, mice, hamsters, gerbils, and guinea pigs are all rodents. In this chapter, you'll find out more about these interesting animals, and the basics of raising them as pets.

Top Five Rodent Facts

• Rodents belong to the order of mammals called *Rodentia*. They're special mammals because they have large, chisel-shaped front teeth for gnawing and cheek teeth for chewing. Rodents eat plants, grains, nuts, seeds, and berries; some eat insects and small animals.

• Nearly half of all the approximately 3,500 species of mammals are rodents.

• Rodents are found worldwide and in almost every kind of habitat, from the shores of the Arctic Ocean to the hottest deserts.

• Different kinds of rodents are adapted for running, jumping, climbing, burrowing, swimming, and gliding. Many use their forepaws like hands to clutch food while sitting on their haunches.

• Most rodents are several inches in length or less. The largest is the Central and South American capybara, which is about 4 feet long and 20 inches high; it weighs 75 to 100 pounds. The smallest wild rodent is the northern pigmy mouse of central Mexico, Arizona, and Texas. It is about 5.3 inches long and weighs 0.24 - 0.35 oz.

Some Well-known Rodents

Rodent	Where Found	Facts & Features
Beaver	Streams and ponds of Asia, Europe, North America	Brown, broad-tailed aquatic rodents, almost as large as the capybara. Beavers gather wood and gnaw small trees to build dams and lodges (houses) of mud and sticks, with entrances below water level and ramps leading to the living area. When danger threatens, a beaver slaps the water loudly with its tail to alert other beavers to scurry to the safety of deeper water.
Chinchilla	The Andes Mountains of South America, at heights of up to 15,000 feet	Burrowing rodent prized for its valuable soft gray pelt. Chinchillas nearly became extinct until protective laws were passed. Now they're raised primarily on farms in South America and the United States.
Chipmunk	Woodlands of Asia, North America	Brown and black-and-white striped rodents that carry their food—nuts, seeds, berries, and insects—in expandable cheek pouches. They store food in burrows for the winter. Chipmunks are excellent climbers.

Rodent	Where Found	Facts & Features
Dormouse	Around bushes and thickets of Africa, Asia, Europe	Brown or gray nocturnal rodent. The name comes from the French word *dormir,* which means "to sleep." Dormice sleep during the day, hibernate for almost 6 months of the year.
Gerbil	Desert regions of Africa and Asia. Popular as pets in the U.S.	Gerbils are sandy, gray, brown, or reddish-colored, and are 3 to 5 inches long. They have long, tufted tails. Wild gerbils get most of their water from desert plants. Most are nocturnal and live in burrows.
Gopher	Meadows and farmlands of Central and North America	Gray, buff, or dark-brown burrowing rodents with very long upper and lower teeth and large claws on their forepaws. A gopher uses its teeth as picks and forepaws as shovels as it tunnels through the ground. Pocket gophers have fur-lined pouches in their cheeks, used for carrying food and nesting material.

Rodent	Where Found	Facts & Features
Groundhog (also called **woodchuck**)	Open woods and ravines of North America	Large (2 feet long) brown rodent. Eats green vegetation and hibernates in burrows. Legend has it that if a groundhog leaves its burrow on February 2 (Groundhog Day) and sees its shadow, there will be 6 more weeks of winter.
Guinea Pig	Europe, North and South America	Often black-and-white or brown short- or long-haired rodents, popular as pets and laboratory animals. Its name comes from the piglike squealing sound it makes.
Hamster	Asia, Europe, North America	Brown-and-white, black-and-white, or golden-and-white nocturnal rodents, popular as pets. Hamsters have cheek pouches for storing food.
Lemming	Tundras and meadows of the Arctic, Northern Asia, Europe, North America	Brown, black, or white burrowing rodents with thick, fluffy fur. Two or three times a decade, the Norway lemming undergoes a huge population boom. Guided by instinct, swarms of lemmings set off in all directions to search for food. They run across land and swim across water in their desperate search. Some reach the ocean, where they drown.

Rodent	Where Found	Facts & Features
Mouse	Meadows and woodlands of Asia, Africa, Europe, North and South America	There are numerous mouse species. The best known are the brown or gray house and field mice, and the all-white albino. The albino is a popular pet and often used for biological and medical experiments. Both house and field mice get into houses, where they may eat food supplies and nest. The nests are made of clothing, paper, and other chewable items. Besides being nuisances, house mice can carry diseases.
Muskrat	Marshes, streams, and ponds of the U.S. and Canada	Aquatic rodents that resemble rats. They have shiny brown fur. Muskrats live in burrows above water level that are connected to an underwater entrance by a tunnel. They eat vegetation and other aquatic animals.
Pack Rat	Woodlands and deserts of Central and North America	Large (18 inches) rodent with soft brown fur. Pack rats are known for their habit of collecting bright shiny objects and replacing them with nuts, pebbles, or other objects.

Rodent	Where Found	Facts & Features
Porcupine	Wooded or scrubby areas of Asia; Africa; Europe; Central, North, and South America	Large, shaggy, brown or black rodents up to 20 inches long and weighing 50 to 60 pounds. The hair of most procupines includes bristles, spines, or quills that pull out easily and can become imbedded in other animals.

Prairie Dog	Prairie and open country of the U.S. and Mexico	Named for their barking cries, these foot-long rodents have short, coarse buff-colored fur. The black-tailed prairie dogs of the U.S. Great Plains live in connecting burrows, forming colonies or "towns" that can stretch for many miles and include thousands of individuals. The entrance to each burrow is topped by a mound of dirt to keep out rainwater.

Rodent	Where Found	Facts & Features
Rat	Rural and suburban areas and cities of Asia; Europe; Central, North, and South America	There are two types of true rats—brown and black. White rats—albinos—are a brown rat strain used in laboratory experiments. The black rat was responsible for spreading the deadly disease called the Bubonic Plague in Europe in the 1300s. Rats are intelligent, adaptable, and aggressive, but they carry diseases and are unwelcome visitors in basements, sewers, attics, and food-storage areas.
Squirrel	Forests, city parks, and suburban areas worldwide except Australia, Madagascar, and Antarctica	Tree-dwelling rodents with slender bodies; sleek, thick fur of black, brown, gray, or red; and bushy tails. Squirrels use their tails as rudders to guide them when they drop from branches and as parachutes when they land. They are light, fast-moving, and agile, with a keen sense of sight and smell. Squirrels use their forepaws to hold food such as nuts, berries, and insects; they sometimes eat eggs, young birds, and smaller mammals. The flying squirrel doesn't really fly—it glides to the ground from branches with the help of furry skin flaps that extend along each side of its body. The flaps stretch out tautly when the animal leaps.

Rodents As Pets

There are three types of furry rodents that make lovable, lively, easy-to-care-for pets: hamsters, gerbils, and guinea pigs. These animals are especially good pets if you live in an apartment or a small house. Some people like to house their pet rodents outside, but the basic information below covers animals that stay indoors, where you can enjoy and care for them more easily.

HAMSTERS AND GERBILS

Buying a Hamster or Gerbil

A pet store is the best place to buy one of these animals. Prices can range from $10 to $20. Make sure you are buying a healthy animal. Check it carefully for signs of hair loss, wounds, or scabs. A hunched-up animal with fur fluffed out may be sick, or have trouble with its teeth.

Housing and Toys

Hamsters live in cages; gerbils live in cages or converted aquariums. Make sure the cage has no rough edges that could injure your pet. It should also be large enough for your pet to scurry around in. The case or aquarium should contain litter and bedding, a water bowl or bottle with a tube, a food bowl, and a few toys. Your gerbil may also like to have a nest box—a small "house" where it can sleep. Gerbils and hamsters like to burrow, so your pet will need enough bedding to dig out a little "room." Safe toys for your gerbil are hollow tubes it can use as tunnels. Your hamster will enjoy running around on an exercise wheel. Make sure the wheel turns smoothly, or else it will squeak. A wheel is *not* a good toy for a gerbil, however; its long tail can get caught and cut. The litter in your pet's cage should be changed at least once a week.

Ask your pet store salesperson to recommend the right kind of housing, bedding, and toys for your hamster or gerbil.

Food

Gerbils and hamsters need fresh water every day. The bowl or bottle should be cleaned daily. There are special feeds for rodents that your pet store salesperson or vet can recommend. Gerbils are often happy on a diet of seeds or pellets, but they should not be fed too many sunflower seeds, which are high in fat. A small amount of greens such as cabbage, lettuce, celery, and watercress are also favorite foods. Bits of carrot, fresh fruit, hard-boiled egg, cheese, or toasted wholewheat bread can be occasional treats. Hamsters like and need fruit, especially apples. Be sure to wash all greens, vegetables, and fruits before feeding them to your pet.

Handling Pet Hamsters and Gerbils

HAMSTERS

Once your hamster is used to you, you should be able to pick it up easily, without worrying that it will nip at your fingers. Lift the hamster gently in your cupped hand and let it walk from one hand to the other. Never turn a hamster over on its back, and never set it free to roam around a room. It will look for a place to hide and can be difficult to find.

GERBILS

Hold the base of the tail with one hand and grip the body with the other hand. Hold the gerbil gently but firmly; gerbils are nimble animals and can escape easily. Never turn a gerbil over on its back.

Be sure to call your vet immediately if your hamster or gerbil seems to be sick.

GUINEA PIGS

Buying a Guinea Pig

The best place to buy a guinea pig is in a pet store. Guinea pigs come in a variety of colors and patterns and can be short-haired or long-haired. Prices range from $10 to $20. Make sure your guinea pig is healthy by checking the eyes and nose. These should be clear and not running. Check the ears for ear mites. Teeth should be straight, and the coat should be bright and shiny. Patches of missing fur indicate poor health. Make sure there are no sores on the underside of the legs.

Housing

Pet stores sell cages, litter, and bedding for guinea pigs. The cage should be about 24 inches long, 18 inches wide, and 12 inches high to give your pet enough room to move around. Keep the cage clean and dry, and change the litter (usually sawdust) twice a week. Your pet's cage should contain a water bottle and food dish. Your guinea pig's cage should be kept away from the hot sun and out of drafts (guinea pigs catch cold and even pneumonia easily).

Food

Prepared guinea pig food can be bought at the pet store. Your pet will also enjoy greens, such as bits of lettuce, celery, or cucumber, as treats. Bits of carrot and apple are another possibility. Some guinea pigs like popcorn, but only one or two kernals should be given, and not very often: this food is hard to digest. It's a good idea to give your guinea pig something to chew on all the time, such as a clean block of wood. This will help to grind down its teeth to keep them from growing too long. Your pet will need fresh water every day.

Handling Your Guinea Pig

Gently lift up your guinea pig with one hand on its hindquarters and the other on its body.

Three Tips on Care

1. If you buy a long-haired guinea pig, such as the Peruvian, be sure to brush it often with a wire dog brush, especially around the tail. Otherwise the tail hair will become matted, preventing your pet from eliminating wastes, which causes illness. You might want to wear rubber gloves when brushing. Guinea pigs don't like to be touched around their tails and may bite.

2. Baths should be given by your vet or at a pet store (this is true for hamsters and gerbils as well), but if you decide to bathe your pet at home, be sure to do it away from drafts.

3. Be sure to call your vet immediately if your guinea pig seems to be sick.

Reptiles and Amphibians

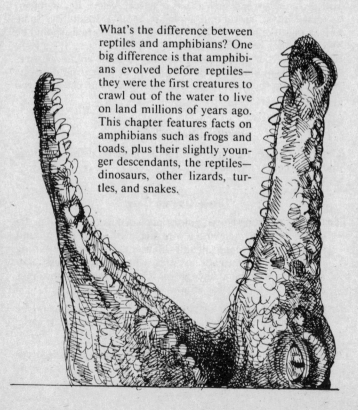

What's the difference between reptiles and amphibians? One big difference is that amphibians evolved before reptiles—they were the first creatures to crawl out of the water to live on land millions of years ago. This chapter features facts on amphibians such as frogs and toads, plus their slightly younger descendants, the reptiles—dinosaurs, other lizards, turtles, and snakes.

Reptiles

Except for snakes and a few lizards, reptiles are cold-blooded four-legged invertebrates. They usually have horny scales, or sometimes bony plates, on their bodies and three to five clawed toes on each foot. Most reptiles lay eggs with hard leathery skins.

HIGHLIGHTS IN THE HISTORY OF REPTILES

• Reptiles evolved from amphibians and made their debut on earth about 250 million years ago. Sixty million years later, they ruled the world. That period is known as the Age of Reptiles.

• There were flying, fishlike, and mammallike reptiles. But by far the largest and best-known primitive reptiles were the dinosaurs (meaning "terrible lizards"). Dinosaur fossils have been found on every continent, including Antarctica.

• Dinosaurs disappeared about 65 million years ago. There are four theories to explain their extinction:

Exploding star—This might have started a heat wave on earth. The weather became too hot for life to survive. Radiation from the exploding star might have killed the dinosaurs or kept them from reproducing.

Meteorite bombardment—Large meteorites may have hit the earth, causing a global fire and/or throwing up clouds of dust that blocked out the sunlight for a long period of time. The earth's climate became too poisonous and cold for the dinosaurs to survive.

Volcanoes—A huge amount of volcanic activity could have destroyed the earth's protective ozone layer. The dinosaurs may have died from exposure to too much deadly ultraviolet radiation from the sun.

Gradual extinction—This is the most widely accepted theory. A series of events such as the temperature and sea-level changes; migration; inability to compete for food with the smaller, faster mammals; and the spread of disease may have caused a slow, not sudden, extinction of the dinosaurs. They simply could not adapt to their changing environment.

Interesting dinosaurs include:

• **BRACHIOSAURUS** (brack-e-o-sore-us), which was 45 feet tall, 80 feet long, and weighed 100,000 pounds.

• **COMPSOGNATHUS** (Comp-sog-nay-thus), the smallest dinosaur. It was about 12 inches long and looked like a bird without feathers. Its nickname is "pretty jaw."

• **DIPLODOCUS** (Diplod-o-cus), at 90 feet long, the second-longest dinosaur.

• **SEISMOSAURUS** (Size-mo-sore-us), the longest and heaviest dinosaur. It was 100 to 120 feet long and weighed at least 89 tons (178,000 pounds). Its nickname is "earthshaker."

• **TYRANNOSAURUS REX** (tie-ran-o-sore-us), the fiercest dinosaur. It had 60 long, sharp teeth, which it used to attack and eat other dinosaurs.

• **ULTRASAURUS** (ultralizard) and **SUPERSAURUS** are new dinosaur discoveries. Both are thought to have been more than five stories high.

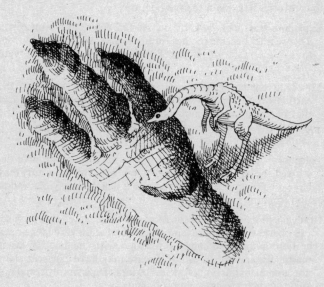

MODERN-DAY REPTILES

Alligators and Crocodiles—Differences and Similarities

Alligator	Crocodile
Has a broad, blunt snout which makes its head look triangular	Has a long, tapering snout. Some of its teeth protrude, like a bulldog's, from each side of its mouth
Adults are black	Adults are paler in color
Prefers freshwater swamps and streams; also lives on banks	Prefers saltwater marshes and will even swim out into the ocean; also lives on river banks
Eats fish, turtles, birds, crayfish, crabs, and other aquatic life	Same diet
Lays eggs that are hatched by the heat of the sun and the rotting vegetation that makes up its nest	Same
Most adults are 9 ft. long	Most adults are 6 to 10 ft. long
Found in warm regions in the Southeastern U.S. and the Gulf states; also China	Found in warm regions in Africa, Southeast Asia, Central and South America, U.S. (Florida), the West Indies
Not usually dangerous	Very dangerous
The American alligator is protected by law	The American crocodile, an endangered species, is also protected by law

LIZARDS

• There are over 5,000 species of lizard throughout the world. They are found on every continent except Antarctica.

• Lizards have adapted to a variety of environments and can be aquatic, terrestrial, subterranean, or arboreal. Most lizards live as far north as Canada and Finland.

• Lizards range in size from three inches or less to the 10-foot-long Komodo Dragon of Southeast Asia.

• These reptiles resemble dinosaurs in looks. Most have four legs, with five toes on each foot, but a few species, such as the worm and legless lizard, are snakelike in appearance: they have long bodies and no legs. Lizards have scaly skin, with rows of scales on the underside of their bodies.

• Lizards have movable eyelids and an ear opening on each side of the head. Their tongues are short and wide, slender and forked, or highly extendable. Lizards use their tongues to "taste" their surroundings as they move along, sending particles from the environment to a sensory organ in the roof of their mouths.

• Lizards eat insects, other small animals, or plants. The horned lizard of the western United States and Mexico snaps its tongue out to catch insects. Lizards are valuable as insect-controllers. They do a much more efficient job of getting rid of insects than insecticides.

• Most lizards lay eggs, but a few types give birth to live young.

• Lizards can run quickly—the fastest has been timed at about 15 miles per hour. Most can swim; some desert species move just below the surface of the sand with a swimming movement.

• The lifespan of some lizards is 54 years; others average less than a year in the wild.

Lizards Found in the United States

GECKOS
Several species of nocturnal lizards with large, lidless eyes having vertical pupils and toes with adhesive pads for climbing vertical surfaces. Colors and patterns include greenish, brownish, spotted, and banded. The tails of these lizards are very brittle and break off easily, but they regrow. Geckos live around houses, on rocks, and in trees, and are found in warm southern states. They eat small insects. Most geckos are gentle lizards that rarely bite.

CHAMELEON
Found in the southeast and the Gulf states, chameleons are also called green anoles. The chameleon has the unique ability to change its color to match its surroundings.

DESERT IGUANA
Also known as the crested lizard, the desert iguana is a large (12 to 15 inches long) spotted and striped lizard with a tail that is almost twice as long as its body. Iguanas live in burrows in the deserts of the Southwest. They feed on desert plants and are timid and harmless.

SPINY LIZARDS
This is a large group of brownish or bluish striped lizards found in most areas of the United States. They are all active during the day and spend the night in crevices, or on branches. Some species lay eggs; others give birth to 6 to 12 live young. Spiny lizards are good climbers.

HORNED LIZARDS
Found only in the western United States and Mexico, horned lizards have a series of hornlike spines on their heads and broad, flat backs. They are green or brown in color. They are found in dry, sandy areas, where they lie on rocks or half-buried in the sand. When frightened, these lizards sometimes squirt a thin stream of blood from the corners of their eyes. Some puff up when angered; others flatten themselves. They hiss threateningly and jump up at an intruder, but their tough act is just that—an act. Horned lizards rarely bite and can be tamed. They are protected in most states.

SKINKS

Greenish or striped skinks are found in most areas of the United States. They are usually not more than five inches long, with a six-inch-long tail. They have smooth, flat scales that look glossy. They eat insects, spiders, and worms. Skinks hibernate all winter in the ground or under logs.

GILA MONSTER

Stay away from this brown-and-black-striped two-foot-long lizard—glands in its lower jaw contain poison. Gila monsters are found in the Southwest. They live under rocks and in burrows by day, and eat eggs, mice, and other lizards. Gila monsters are slow and clumsy creatures, but they can twist their heads, bite quickly, and hang on to their prey with a great deal of strength. It is against the law to catch or hurt Gila monsters, which are the only venomous lizards in the United States.

SNAKES

• Snakes are elongated, limbless reptiles with horny scales covering their skins. Young snakes shed and regrow their skins at least once, and often several times a year, for two or three years. Most have protective coloring that blends in with their surroundings.

• Snakes are related to lizards, but they do not have ear openings and moving eyelids. They do have keen eyesight for short distances, but poor long-distance vision. Some can see well at night. Instead of hearing, snakes pick up vibrations that travel from the ground to the bones of the skull. They are deaf to sound carried by air.

• Snakes have forked tongues which they use to sense their surroundings as they slither along, sending particles from the environment to a sensory organ in the roof of their mouths.

• Some snakes have two lungs for breathing; others have one lung. These reptiles have no larynx or voice box, but they can make a hissing sound. They slither along by contracting and extending their muscles.

• Most snakes live on the ground; some are burrowers. Others live in trees or are aquatic. Snakes that live in temperate climates hibernate.

• Usually solitary animals, snakes sometimes get together for food or shelter, and large numbers may hibernate together.

• Snakes range in length from about four inches (the thread snake) to over 30 feet (the reticulated, or royal, python).

• Snakes eat insects, worms, frogs, mice, rats, rabbits, and sometimes other snakes. Their teeth are designed for catching their prey, but not for chewing; they swallow their food whole. The large constrictor snakes wrap their bodies around their prey, squeezing it to death. Venomous snakes inject poison into their victims.

• Some snakes lay eggs; others give birth to live young.

• There are about 2,700 snake species throughout the world. Snakes are found on every continent except Antarctica.

Seven Well-Known Snakes

BOA

The members of this snake family have two lungs and hind leg bones that end in external horny claws. Boas catch prey with their teeth, squeeze it to death, and swallow it whole. Boas can be terrestrial, arboreal, or burrowers. The best known is probably the dark-brown, diamond-backed *boa constrictor,* found from Mexico to Argentina. Its length is usually 6 to 9 feet, but it sometimes reaches lengths of 14 feet. The 2- to 3-foot-long striped *rosy boa* and the grayish *rubber boa* are found in the western United States and southwest Canada. The South American *anaconda* is the longest boa and the thickest snake. It can reach 25 feet in length and is often 3 feet thick. Anacondas live in or near streams and river shallows, where they lie in wait for animals that come to drink.

COBRA

This venomous snake is found in Africa and Asia. Cobras have short, rigid fangs attached to the front of their mouths, and neck hoods. The hood is made up of loose skin around the neck. When a cobra is threatened or excited, it spreads its hood and inflates it with air from its lungs. Cobras hunt at night and eat small mammals, birds, and frogs. The king cobra of Southeast Asia is the largest venomous snake, often reaching lengths of 18 feet. Its preferred food is other snakes. The Indian cobra is found in the same region. It is usually 4 to 5 feet long. The back of its large hood is decorated with a pattern of figures that look like eyes. This cobra feeds on rats and often enters houses.

COPPERHEAD, COTTONMOUTH

These are two venomous snake species that are related to rattlesnakes. They are found in the eastern United States and the Gulf states. Copperheads have a coppery-colored head and body patches. They are 30 to 50 inches long. Dark-colored, swamp-dwelling cottonmouths are 40 to 58 inches long and are heavier and more vicious than copperheads. Both snakes have a pit between their eyes and nostrils that is sensitive to heat. This pit helps them locate and strike at their warm-blooded prey. Cottonmouths are also known as water moccasins.

GARTER SNAKE

This is the most common snake found in the United States, Canada, and Central America. Garter snakes are harmless striped or banded snakes that eat frogs, toads, and earthworms. They give birth to live young, as many as 20 or more at one time. Garter snakes range in length from 18 to 44 inches.

PYTHON

This type of constrictor is found in tropical forests of Africa, Asia, Australia, and the South Pacific. The reticulated or royal python or Southeast Asia, Indonesia, and the Philippines can reach lengths of 30 feet or more. It is the longest snake in the world. It is found in towns as well as in forests. Pythons are good swimmers and climbers, and they eat birds and mammals.

RATTLESNAKE

There are 15 species of this dangerous venomous snake. Rattlers are found in North and South America. They range in length from 18 inches (the pygmy rattler) to 6 feet (the timber rattler). These snakes have a "rattle" at the end of their bodies, made up of a series of dried, hollow segments of skin. When rattlers are alarmed, they shake their rattles, which give off a whirring sound. However, the rattle of the extremely bad-tempered pigmy rattler can barely be heard. The best-known rattlesnakes are probably the diamondbacks, found in the southwestern and southeastern United States, and the sidewinder, found in the deserts of the Southwest. The sidewinder slithers sideways across the sand. The eastern diamondback is the largest (5 to 9 feet long) and the deadliest rattlesnake. Rattlesnakes give birth to live young; their venom is deadly, even at birth.

Venomous Snakes of the World

Stay away from these poisonous creatures, and never, *ever* walk barefoot or wear sandals in areas where there are snakes. Starred (*) snakes can be found in the United States.

Asian Pit Viper

Australian Brown Snake

Barba Amerilla

Black Mamba

Boomslang

Bushmaster

Cobra

Copperhead*

Coral Snake*

Cottonmouth*

Death Adder

Desert Horned Viper

European Vipers

Gaboon Viper (longest fangs; early 2 in. long)

Krait

Puff Adder

Rattlesnake*

Russell's Viper

Saw-scaled or Carpet Viper

Sea Snake (most venomous)

Sharp-nosed Pit Viper

Taipan

Tiger Snake

TURTLES, TORTOISES, AND TERRAPINS

• Tortoises and terrapins are two species of turtle. **Tortoises** are turtles that live on land all the time. **Terrapins** are freshwater turtles that are edible. All other fresh- and saltwater species are called turtles. The aquatic turtles have webbed feet.

• Turtles appeared about **200 million years** ago, long before the dinosaur. They have managed to survive, relatively unchanged in appearance, for at least 150 million years. There are some **265 kinds** of turtles.

• Turtles have **armorlike shells** and beaked, **horny jaws** instead of teeth. The upper part of the shell is called the **carapace.** It covers the turtle's back and sides. The lower part of the shell, called the **plastron,** covers the underside of the animal. The shells are joined at the sides. Most turtles can pull their necks, heads, and tails into their shells for protection. They have lungs for breathing.

• Turtles are found in most temperate and tropical areas of the world. Only **side-necked** turtles (a turtle that swings its head sideways and tucks it next to its shoulder) are found in Australia.

• All turtles lay their **eggs** on land, burying them in the ground. It takes five to seven years for a newly hatched turtle to grow to adulthood.

• Turtles range in **length** from **three inches** (spotted and bog turtles) to **over eight feet** (leatherback turtle).

• These reptiles are the **longest-lived animals.** Many turtles have lived for over 50 years and some up to 150 years.

• Most turtles eat both **plant and animal food,** including insects, worms, grubs, shellfish, fish, and some fruits and plants. Some turtles are herbivorous.

Some Turtles of the United States

BOX TURTLES

These four- to five-inch turtles live in moist, open woods or swamps. There are two species, Eastern and Western. They eat insects, earthworms, snails, fruits, and berries. Box turtles have a hinged plastron which they pull tight for complete protection when they are frightened.

PAINTED TURTLES

These five- to six-inch turtles are found by streams, ponds, swamps, or ditches in most areas. They feed on water plants, insects, and other small animals. They are also scavengers. Painted turtles can often be seen in groups sunning themselves on logs, rocks, or floating water plants. This turtle's carapace is dark-colored with a red edge; its plastron is yellow, or yellow and red. Painted turtles are shy and like to be left alone, but they aren't bad-tempered.

SEA TURTLES

Sea turtles are found in warm waters of the Atlantic and Pacific Oceans. The legs of these marine turtles have been modified into flippers without toes, streamlined for swimming. Sea turtles can't move very well on shore and spend most of their time in the water. They come ashore in the late spring to lay their eggs. Their heads are too large to retract into their shells. The green sea turtle is a greenish- to brownish-colored turtle about four feet long that weighs about 500 pounds. It eats marine vegetation and is usually found in shallow water. The loggerhead is a large-headed brown to reddish carnivorous sea turtle that lives in open oceans, coastal salt marshes, and the mouths of streams. Both the loggerhead and the green turtle sometimes come ashore to bask in the sun. The hawksbill, or tortoiseshell, sea turtle is prized for its beautiful brown and yellow shell, often made into combs or ornamental objects. The leatherback—the largest of all turtles—weighs in at close to 1,500 pounds. It has a ridged, leathery back.

SNAPPING TURTLE

This vicious turtle and its equally dangerous relative, the alligator snapping turtle, live in quiet, muddy water. Snappers have long necks and powerful jaws, and can deliver painful bites. Both types

of snappers eat fish and sometimes waterfowl. The alligator has three high ridges on its back. It lies on the muddy bottom of a pond wiggling a pink, wormlike growth on its tongue to attract unwary fish. The alligator is found around the Gulf states; the snapping turtle is found throughout the eastern United States.

TORTOISE
These land turtles have blunt, club-shaped feet for walking on land. Tortoises are found in southern areas. The largest land turtle, the giant tortoise, lives in the Indian Ocean and the Galápagos Islands. Giant tortoises can reach lengths of over four feet and weights of over 500 pounds. Tortoises eat insects, small animals, and plants. Most are burrowers.

TERRAPIN
Terrapins are sometimes called diamondbacks, because of the angular rings on their carapaces. These web-footed turtles were once raised for food on turtle farms, but their popularity as a delicacy has declined. Young terrapins are now protected by law. Terrapins are found on the Atlantic and Gulf coasts in brackish (salty) water and tidewater streams. They eat small shellfish, crabs, worms, and plants.

Amphibians

• These cold-blooded vertebrates evolved after fish and before reptiles. Amphibians were the first animals to crawl out of the water to live on land.

• Modern-day amphibians are not well adapted to a full-time life on land. Most adults spend at least part of the time in water or in moist surroundings, but they need air to survive.

• There are three types of amphibians: frogs and toads, salamanders, and caecilians. Caecilians are a little-known tropical group of primitive amphibians that resemble earthworms. These burrowing animals are legless, nearly tailless, earless, and almost or completely blind.

• Most amphibians have four legs; some have two legs. All have smooth or warty skin, which is usually damp. They lay jelly-covered eggs in water. The eggs of frogs and toads hatch into legless larvae, called tadpoles, which breathe through gills and spend their babyhood completely in water. Tadpoles feed on microscopic plants. Baby salamanders, called larvae, are hatched with legs.

• Adult amphibians eat chiefly insects. In northern regions, they hibernate underground or in mud on pond bottoms during the winter.

• The word *amphibia* means "double life." It refers to the ability of amphibians to live in water and on land at different times.

FROGS AND TOADS

There are about **2,700 frog and toad species** throughout the world. They are found in temperate and tropical regions and on every continent except Antarctica. Frogs and toads do not inhabit permanently snowcapped mountains, waterless deserts, some of the Pacific islands, or lands north of the Arctic Circle.

• True **toads** usually have short legs, plump bodies, and rough or warty skin. They live mainly on land. Toads move more slowly than frogs and cannot jump as well. **Frogs** have slender, streamlined bodies, long legs, and smoother skins. They live in water or wet areas.

• Most male frogs and toads have a sac in their throat that inflates when they make their well-known "ribbit, ribbit" **sounds.** Many frogs also make trilling, chirping, or clicking sounds.

• Toads are essentially **harmless.** They were once thought to cause warts, but this has been found *not* to be true. However, true toads may secrete a white fluid that can be very poisonous if it comes into contact with the eyes or mouth.

• Frogs and toads have protrusible **tongues,** which means that they can snap them out to catch their favorite food—insects.

• Frogs can be black, brown, reddish, or green in **color;** toad colors are black, brown, grayish, greenish, or pink. They range in **size** from ¾ inch (cricket frogs) to 7½ inches (bullfrogs).

• Well-known frogs found in the **United States** include tree, chorus, green, leopard, wood, spotted, and bullfrogs.

• Toads found in the United States are true toads, spadefoot, and narrowmouth.

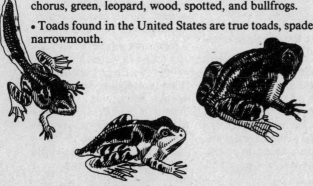

SALAMANDERS

• Salamanders are nocturnal, scaleless, clawless, long-bodied, tailed amphibians. They are found in parts of Africa; northern South America; Asia; Europe; and Central and North America. The greatest number of salamanders are found in North America. There are some **240 different kinds** of salamander.

• Salamanders need **moisture** on their bodies at all times. Most live on land, under damp forest debris. In dry weather, they move into a hole or crevice to find moisture.

• A few kinds of salamanders are **arboreal**: They live in plants that grow on trees in tropical forests, or in knotholes of trees in temperate zones. Some are **aquatic** and never leave the water. They are found in rivers, ponds, brooks, swamps, and streams. Others spend their lives in dark caves. These **subterranean** salamanders are nearly or completely blind.

• Salamanders range in **size** from 2½ inches (four-toed salamander) to 36 inches (*amphiumas*).

• Salamanders lay their jelly-coated **eggs** singly or in clumps or rows in standing water or damp soil.

• Salamanders **eat insects and worms.** Some are colored to blend in with rocks and moss.

• **Newts** are a type of salamander found in woods and ponds of the Northern Hemisphere. They are about three to five inches long and are dark brown or reddish in color. The larvae of some newts leave the water to spend two or three years on land. These little newts are called red **efts.**

Insects and Spiders

Wait! Before you go "Eeuuw!" and start getting shivers up and down your spine, read on. These little creatures are interesting animals. Really. Ants are hard workers, ladybugs are pretty, fireflies are fun to watch on a summer evening, and spiders weave beautiful webs. Some people even think a spider in the house (a nonpoisonous spider of course) brings good luck. So give bugs a chance. (And, anyway, it's a short chapter.)

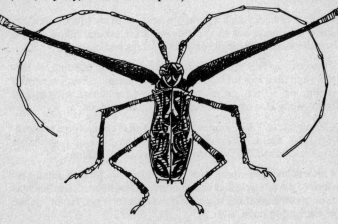

Insects

• Insects first appeared on earth about 200 million years ago and are likely to survive for many more millions of years. The ancestor of insects was probably a segmented wormlike creature. Fossil records show that most insects have changed very little in looks over the centuries.

• There are over a million species of insect—it's the largest group of animals in the world. Insects are found in every country and on every continent, even the Antarctic. Nearly all insects live in every kind of habitat except the sea (there is one marine species, the water spider).

• Insects are invertebrates, which means they have no backbone. Like their relatives, crabs and lobsters, insects have a kind of skeleton *outside* of their bodies, called an exoskeleton.

• The bodies of insects are made up of three parts—the head, thorax, and abdomen. Each of an insect's six jointed legs is attached to the thorax, just behind the head. Most insects also have two pairs of wings attached to the thorax. Some only have one pair of wings, and a few insects are wingless.

• Insects also have two sets of jaws, two kinds of eyes, and a pair of antennae.

• Bugs breathe through a complex network of air tubes called tracheae that open out to the sides of their bodies. Some species breathe directly through the walls of their bodies.

• Insects use their mouths for chewing, sucking, piercing, or lapping, and their legs for walking, running, jumping, burrowing, and swimming. Insects eat plants or decaying material, such as garbage. Many also eat other insects or small animals.

• Many insects have shapes and colors that camouflage and protect them against their enemies. Some have stinging spines or hairs and harmful secretions that they use for defense.

• Insects lay eggs. Some eggs hatch into fully formed small versions of the adult, called young or nymphs. Other insects, such as flies, go through three stages of development: eggs, larvae, pupae or the resting stage, adult.

• Insects can be annoying and sometimes dangerous pests. Some are disease carriers (flies, fleas, mosquitos, and ticks), and others sting (bees, wasps, hornets, and some ants). But many insects help humans by preying on harmful insect species, and others, such as scarab beetles, or help farmers by aerating soil. Insects also provide food for animals such as reptiles, amphibians, and birds.

BUG BITES

• **Katydids,** brown, green, or pink-colored insects, hear through "ears" on the upper parts of their front legs. Their call gives them their name.

• The well-known brown American **cockroach** is found throughout the U.S. It prefers moist, dark places and usually comes out at night. A southern species of cockroach, the palmetto bug, is frequently seen flying.

• **Praying mantises** are so named because the front legs of these slender green or brown insects are bent together in a "praying" position.

• Swarms of **grasshoppers** and **locusts** sometimes destroy crops, especially in the western United States, but they also serve as food for large birds, small mammals, and other animals. (For an amazing account of a "plague" of grasshoppers, read *On the Banks of Plum Creek,* a *Little House* book by Laura Ingalls Wilder.)

• **Termites** live in colonies with a king, queen, and soldiers. Termites feed on wood and can do a great deal of damage to houses and other buildings if they are not controlled.

• **Cicadas** are often heard, steadily humming, in late summer. Males make the noise, using platelike organs on their thoraxes. Most cicadas live for only a few weeks—long enough to breed.

• **Dragonflies,** long thin flying insects with filmy wings, are often seen near ponds and damp meadows. They are popularly known as "darning needles."

• **Butterflies and moths** are the largest and prettiest insects. Both hatch into larvae called caterpillars, and both have beautiful, wide, multicolored and patterned wings as adults. Butterflies usually fly by day, and have thin antennae ending in a knob. Moths fly by night, rest with their wings in a horizontal position, and often have feathery antennae. Both eat plants. The silk of alianthus silkmoths comes from their cocoons.

• **Flies** are known as disease carriers and pests, but one type, the black horse fly, bites. Black horse flies are sometimes an inch long.

• **Fruit flies** live for less than two weeks, but these tiny (about 0.2 inches) insects have been important in laboratory experiments, especially on heredity.

• If the eyed **click beetle** falls or lands on its back, it rests for a moment. Then, with a loud "click," it flips into the air. If it is lucky enough to land on its feet, it runs away. If not, it tries again.

• **Ladybugs**—round, reddish beetles with spots on their backs—are also called ladybird beetles. Ladybugs are important to citrus farmers because they eat insects that damage citrus trees.

• **Ants** are social animals, living and working together in nests and burrows. There are over 15,000 ant species, making ants the most numerous insects on earth. The best known are the carpenter ants, fire ants, and various small black ants. Two tropical species, the fierce army and driver ants, travel in broad bands by thousands, overrunning and devouring insects and even large animals that cannot flee their path.

• **Bees** are hairy insects that live in hives consisting of queens, workers, and drones. Bumblebees are the largest kind—about one inch long—and the only bees that can pollinate red clover. The 0.5 inch-long honeybee is probably the best known. Honey is made by bees from the nectar of flowers. The nectar is taken from the flower by workers and carried in honey sacs back to the hive, where the workers move their wings to circulate the air, which evaporates excess water. This causes honey to be formed from the nectar. Drones exist for the sole purpose of fertilizing eggs.

TOP SIX SPIDER FACTS

• Spiders are similar to insects, but they are classed as *arachnids,* meaning that they have two body parts—the cephalothroax and the abdomen—eight legs, and no antennae.

• Spiders have two pairs of appendages on the undersides of their heads. They use one pair to catch and paralyze prey, injecting it with venom produced in poison glands.

• Spiders also have three pairs of spinnerets, located toward the tip of the abdomen. The spinnerets produce protein-packed fluids that harden as they are pulled out for silk threads. Spiders use these threads to build cocoons, eggs sacs, and webs, or to immobilize their prey. Strands are also spun out for ballooning or floating.

• Spiders eat insects; some large species ensnare and kill small snakes, birds, and mammals. Many spiders will eat each other.

• Young spiders can regrow missing legs or parts of legs.

• Several spiders have bites that are very painful or dangerous to humans. The most venomous spiders are:

Atrax—Large spider varieties found in Australia.

Black Widow—Small, round-bodied spider with hourglass markings. Found around the world in tropical and temperate regions.

Brown, Fiddleback, or Recluse—Small, oval-shaped spiders found throughout the United States.

Tarantula—Various large, hairy, chiefly tropical spiders capable of inflicting a painful but not seriously poisonous bite.

A venomous relative of the spider is the *scorpion,* a crablike arachnid with a stinger in its tail. Scorpions are found in tropical and subtropical areas around the world.

INSECT AND SPIDER CHAMPS

Longest
The giant stick-insect of Indonesia.
Length: 13 in.

Smallest
Hairy-winged beetles and battledore-winged fairy flies are smaller than some protozoa (one-celled animals).

Heaviest
Goliath beetles of Africa.
Weight: 2.5 to 3.5 oz.

Loudest
The cicada, whose call can be heard for over a quarter of a mile.

Most Honey
A hive in Australia yielded 549 lbs. of honey in 1983.

Largest cockroach
The giant burrowing cockroach of Australia.
Length: 3 ft., 11 in.
Width: 1 ft., 49 in.
Weight: 0.77 oz.

Largest Butterfly
The protected Queen Alexandria birdwing of Papua New Guinea.
Wingspan: over 11.02 in.
Weight: over 0.88 oz.

Smallest Butterfly
The *Micropsyche ariana*
Wingspan: 0.275 in.

Rarest Butterfly
The birdwing of the Solomon Islands, of which fewer than 12 are known to exist.

Largest Spider
The Goliath bird-eating spider of northern South America
Length: 4 in.
Leg Span: 10½ in.
Length of fangs: 1 in.
Weight: 4.35 oz.

Smallest Spider
The *Patu marplesi* of Western Samoa
Overall size: 0.016 in. (half the size of the period at the end of this sentence).

Largest Spider Webs
The webs of the tropical orb weavers, which measure 18 ft., 9-¾ in. in circumference

Smallest Spider Webs
A number of spiders spin webs that span less than ¾ of an inch.

Most Venomous Spider
The Brazilian wandering spider of South America, which often enters human dwellings and hides in clothing or shoes.

Rarest Spider
The trapdoor spiders of Southeast Asia, which are seldom seen.

Animals in the Media

Animals have always been favorite characters in stories. Here are some of the best and most popular animal books, movies, and prime-time TV shows, plus a lineup of magazines about animals.

Books About Animals

(FICTION)

ABEL'S ISLAND
William Steig
An elegant, leisure-loving mouse becomes stranded on a river island, where he learns to develop his survival skills and gains a deeper understanding of the meaning of life.

BLACK BEAUTY
Anna Sewell
The classic 19th-century tale of a beautiful horse's experiences at the hands of many owners, ranging from the kind-hearted Squire Gordon to a cruel cab driver.

THE BLACK STALLION STORIES
Walter Farley
A popular series of books featuring a beautiful Arab stallion and the fillies and colts he sires.

BUNNICULA
Deborah and James Howe
Harold, the Monroe's dog, tells of Chester the Cat's suspicions that the baby rabbit that one of the Monroe boys finds in the movie theater, takes home, and names Bunnicula, is a vampire. *Howliday Inn* is another book that features Harold and Chester.

CHARLOTTE'S WEB
E.B. White
The life of Wilbur the pig is saved, first by a tenderhearted girl named Fern Arable, and then by Wilbur's best friend, Charlotte, a spider who weaves wonderful messages in her web. This book features a barnyard of interesting characters, including a scheming rat named Templeton.

THE CRICKET IN TIMES SQUARE
George Selden
Chester Cricket is carried in a picnic basket from rural Connecticut to New York's Times Square. There he makes some surprising friends and learns about life in the city.

THE FLEDGLING
Jane Langton
A great Canadian goose helps eight-year-old Georgie learn to fly in this fantasy.

THE INCREDIBLE JOURNEY
Sheila Burnford
The story of two dogs and a cat who make the long journey through the wilds of Canada back to their home.

JENNY AND THE CAT CLUB
Esther Averill
Stories featuring Jenny Linsky, a small black cat who joins the neighborhood cat club and has many interesting adventures.

JULIE OF THE WOLVES
Jean Craighead George
When a 13-year-old Eskimo girl runs away from home and gets lost on the wild North Slope of Alaska, she wins the trust of a pack of Arctic wolves.

THE JUNGLE BOOKS
Rudyard Kipling
These stories feature Mowgli, a boy who has been brought up in the jungles of India by a pack of wolves. Other stories feature animals such as Rikki-Tikki-Tavi, a pet mongoose who heroically fights the deadly cobras that threaten the family he lives with.

THE LINDA CRAIG SERIES
Ann Sheldon
A series of books set on a sprawling California ranch and featuring Linda Craig and her golden palomino, Amber.

LIZARD MUSIC
Daniel Manus Pinkwater
The zany adventures of a young sci-fi lover who travels to an island inhabited by a colony of charming lizards.

THE MARGUERITE HENRY BOOKS
This author's books about horses are among kids' all-time favorites. Some of her most popular books are *King of the Wind,* the sto-

ry of an Arab stallion and the boy who looks after him; *Justin Morgan Had a Horse,* the story of the Morgan horse; *Brighty of the Grand Canyon,* about a burro who lives in the Grand Canyon; and *Misty of Chincoteague,* featuring a wild pony of Chincoteague Island.

THE MOUSE AND THE MOTORCYCLE
Beverly Cleary
Reckless young Ralph Mouse makes friends with the boy in Room 215 of the Mountainview Inn and discovers the joys of motorcycling.

MRS. FRISBY AND THE RATS OF NIMH
Robert C. O'Brien
A widowed mouse seeks help from a group of superintelligent, long-lived laboratory rats when her home and family are threatened.

OLIVER AND COMPANY
Michael McBrier
A series of books about 12-year-old Oliver Moffitt, who runs a pet-sitting business. Besides the usual dogs, cats, and birds, Oliver's clients include a goat, a snake, and an alligator.

THE RUNAWAYS
Victor Canning
A 15-year-old runaway boy and an escaped cheetah share the same hideout in this exciting, heartwarming novel.

SASHA, MY FRIEND
Barbara Corcoran
Fifteen-year-old Hallie hates living on a Christmas tree farm in Montana—until she finds and tames a wolf cub. (Arrow Book Club title: *My Wolf, My Friend.*)

STUART LITTLE
E. B. White
A smart, resourceful mouse, the son of human parents, has a number of unusual adventures in and around his New York City home before deciding to travel and see the world.

THE TWO OF A KIND SERIES
Molly Albright
The hilarious and heartwarming adventures of spunky, 12-year-old Melissa Fremont and her huge, lovable Old English sheepdog, Baby.

WATERSHIP DOWN
Richard Adams
A group of rabbits flee their warren when it is destroyed to make way for a building site and begin a long journey to find a new, safe home.

THE WIND IN THE WILLOWS
Kenneth Grahame
The classic story of the adventures of Rat, Mole, and Toad of Toad Hall.

THE YEARLING
Marjorie Kinnan Rawlings
A 12-year-old Florida boy, Jody Baxter, tames a fawn named Flag, who becomes his special pet.

Movies About Animals

Benji (1974)

The first of four movies starring Benji, a lovable little stray dog who saves two kidnapped children. Sequels are *For the Love of Benji*, *Oh, Heavenly Dog*, and *Benji, the Hunted*.

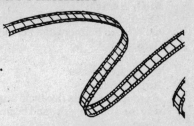

The Black Stallion (1979)

Based on the book by Walter Farley, this well-made movie tells the story of a young boy's adventures with a beautiful stallion—from a shipwreck to a racing championship. *The Black Stallion Returns* was a 1983 sequel.

Charlie, the Lonesome Cougar (1968)

This Disney adventure/comedy features a friendly cougar who lives in a lumber camp.

Clarence, the Cross-Eyed Lion (1965)

Clarence is just one of many animal characters in this humorous movie about an American veterinarian who runs an animal study center in Africa.

Ride a Wild Pony (1976)

This Australian movie tells the story of a lovable pony and the two children—one poor, one rich and disabled—who compete for the pony's love and ownership.

The Three Lives of Thomasina (1964)

Thomasina is a much-loved yellow tabby that belongs to the daughter of a heartless Scottish veterinarian. Their lives are totally changed by a pretty young woman who doctors animals with love and her own special kind of healing.

Lassie Come Home (1943)

After a poor family is forced to sell their beloved collie, the dog sets off on a difficult and dangerous journey to get back to them. A remake of this movie, *The Magic of Lassie*, came out in 1978.

Old Yeller (1957)

A yellow hunting dog becomes the beloved pet of a Texas boy in this Disney movie. Based on the popular novel by Fred Gipson.

Dusty (1982)

This is a heartwarming Australian movie about a dingo (wild dog) captured as a pup and raised by an elderly man.

The Shaggy Dog (1959)

Slapstick Disney fantasy/comedy about a boy who turns into a sheepdog as the result of an ancient spell and catches some crooks. *The Shaggy D.A.* was a 1976 sequel, and there was a 1987 made-for-TV movie, *The Return of the Shaggy Dog.*

The Journey of Natty Gann (1985)

During the 1930s, a girl travels cross-country during the hardest days of the Depression so that she can be with her father. A wolf she meets along the way becomes her companion and protector.

National Velvet (1944)

A very young Elizabeth Taylor starred in this excellent movie about British kids determined to train their horse to win the famous Grand National Steeplechase. A sequel, *International Velvet,* came out in 1978 and starred Tatum O'Neal.

Ring of Bright Water (1969)

The heartwarming story of a man who lives in the Scottish Highlands with his pet otter.

The Ugly Dachshund (1966)

This fast-moving Disney comedy features a married couple who train their dogs for a competition. The title refers to an orphaned Great Dane puppy who is nurtured by a female dachshund with her own puppies.

That Darn Cat (1965)

Smart but mischievous D.C. (Darn Cat) leads an FBI man on the trail of a woman kidnapped by bank robbers in this Disney comedy/thriller.

TV Shows About Animals

Some of these shows are on the air in reruns from time to time, so check your local listings.

"All Creatures Great and Small"

This British series about the experiences of James Herriot, a vet in the county of Yorkshire, first aired on public television in the 1970s. Based on the books by real-life vet James Herriot. Also shown on the Arts and Entertainment cable channel.

"Black Beauty"

Based on the classic story by Anna Sewell, this series was first aired on PBS and has been rerun on the Arts and Entertainment and Disney cable channels.

"Daktari"

Based on the 1965 movie *Clarence, the Cross-Eyed Lion,* this series features an American veterinarian and his daughter who ran an animal study center in Africa. It aired from 1966 to 1969. ("Daktari" is an African word meaning doctor.) Dr. Tracy and his daughter, Paula, had two pets, a lion named Clarence, and Judy, a chimpanzee.

"Flipper"

This series, set in Florida, was on the air from 1964 to 1968 and focused on the adventures of brothers Sandy and Bud and their pet dolphin, Flipper. The role of Flipper was played by a dolphin named Suzy.

"Gentle Ben"

Ben was a 650-pound American black bear who was as friendly and lovable as he was huge. He lived with Tom and Ellen Wedloe and their eight-year-old son, Mark, in the Florida Everglades, where Tom was a wildlife officer. This series was on the air from 1967 to 1969.

"Lassie"

One of the longest-running series in TV history (1954-1971), "Lassie" featured a brave, loyal, supersmart collie who was constantly involved in exciting adventures. This canine heroine lived with a variety of owners, including Jeff Miller, his mother, and grandfather; Timmy Martin and his parents; and Corey Stuart, a forest ranger. "Lassie" is often shown in reruns.

"Mr. Ed"

A talking horse? Of course, of course! This silly, sometimes amusing situation comedy lasted form 1961 to 1965 and featured a palomino who could talk—but he would only talk to his owner, Wilbur Post. Mr. Ed got Wilbur into a number of zany and uncomfortable situations with his wife, neighbors, and boss. "Mr. Ed" is currently seen on The Nickleodeon cable channel.

"National Velvet"

This adventure series based on the movie of the same name ran from 1960 to 1962. It starred Lori Martin as 12-year-old Velvet Brown, who hopes to train her beautiful chestnut thoroughbred, King, to race in the Grand National Steeplechase. Currently shown in reruns on the TNT cable channel.

PBS Nature Shows

If you like to watch documentary shows about animals in the wild, your public television station is the one to tune in. PBS offers a wide variety of good shows about all kinds of animals.

"Rin Tin Tin"

"Rinty" was a smart, heroic German shepherd who lived with the soldiers of Fort Apache, Arizona, in the late 1800s. He was the pet of an orphaned boy, Rusty, who had been adopted by the soldiers. Rusty and Rinty helped the cavalry and the townspeople of the nearby town of Mesa Grande keep law and order in the Old West. "Rin Tin Tin" was on the air from 1954 to 1959, and has been shown in reruns since 1959.

"Sergeant Preston of the Yukon"

This adventure series ran from 1955 to 1958. Sergeant Preston was an officer of the Canadian Royal Northwest Mounted Police (Mounties) who brought law and order to the wild Yukon Territory of Canda. His two main helpers were Yukon King, a mega-intelligent Malamute dog, and Rex, a well-trained black horse.

Magazines About Animals

Starred magazines (*) can be purchased at newsstands, as well as by subscription.

ANIMALS* (bimonthly, $15/year)
Massachusetts Society for the Prevention of Cruelty to Animals
350 South Huntington Avenue
Boston, MA 02130

FEATURES: Articles and special reports on domestic and wild animals. Includes regular features on endangered animals, animal health, and current animal news.

BIRD TALK* (monthly, $19.97/year)
P.O. Box 6040
Mission Viejo, CA 92690 9953

FEATURES: Articles on birds. Includes regular features on health, nutrition, and training, and a color centerfold.

CAT FANCY* (monthly, $19.97/year)
P.O. Box 52864
Boulder, CO 80322-2864

FEATURES: Articles on cats. Includes current cat news, shopping section, show calendar, and a section just for kids entitled "Kids for Cats."

CATS* (monthly, $18.50/year)
P.O. Box 83048
Lincoln, NE 68501

FEATURES: Articles on cats, a show calendar, and regular columns such as *Let's Talk Cats, Tails n' Tales, What's Mew,* and *The Question Box.*

DOG FANCY* (monthly, $19.97/year)
P.O. Box 53264
Boulder, CO 80322-3264

FEATURES: Articles on dogs. Includes regular columns such as *Pupourri, On Good Behavior, Pets and People, Puppy Love,* a column on purebreds, current dog news, and a show calendar.

HORSE ILLUSTRATED* (monthly, $17.97/first 12 issues)
P.O. Box 6040
Mission Viejo, CA 92690-9983

FEATURES: Articles on horses. Includes columns on training, showing, tack, first aid; and features horse stories.

NATIONAL GEOGRAPHIC WORLD (monthly $10.95/year)
Department 00189
17th and M Sts. NW
Washington, DC 20036

FEATURES: Articles on animals around the world. Includes features such as Far-Out Facts, Prehistoric Mailbag, and What in the World?

OUR FOURFOOTED FRIENDS (4 times a year, $4/year)
Animal Rescue League of Boston
P.O. Box 265
Boston, MA 02117-0265

FEATURES: Articles on all kinds of animals and pets.

RANGER RICK'S NATURE MAGAZINE (monthly, $14/year)
National Wildlife Federation
1412 16th St. NW
Washington, D.C. 20036

FEATURES: Articles on wildlife.

More About Pet Care

This chapter features general information on pet care: cold and hot weather tips, first aid, how to find a lost pet, and more.

Cold Weather Tips

• Keep your cat inside, especially during the coldest part of the winter. Cats can easily bog down in the snow and freeze, or become lost.

• Take your dog outside only long enough to relieve itself. Dogs, especially small, short-haired breeds, suffer from the cold. You might want to get your dog a warm sweater for cold winter months. Make sure it fits snugly.

• Never let your dog off the leash on snow or ice, especially during a snowstorm. Dogs often lose their sense of smell in icy weather and easily become lost. They may also panic during a snowstorm and run away. More dogs are lost during the winter than during any other season.

• Never leave your dog or cat alone in a car during cold weather. A car can act like a refrigerator, holding in the cold. Your pet could freeze to death.

• Wipe off your dog's legs and stomach throughly when it comes in out of the rain, snow, or ice. Check your dog's sensitive foot pads to make sure they aren't bleeding from snow or ice encrusted in them. Your dog may also pick up salt and other chemicals on its feet, which can hurt your pet if it swallows them while licking its feet.

• Increase your pet's supply of food, especially protein to keep its fur thick and healthy. Ask your vet about an increased diet and vitamin and oil supplements.

• Make sure your pet has a warm place to sleep far away from drafts and preferably off the floor.

• Give your dog a bath only when it's absolutely necessary. A dog can catch a cold anytime it gets wet. You might want to consider having a professional dog bather give your dog a bath instead.

• Never clip your dog's hair in the winter—brush your pet daily instead. Your dog will stay warmer and will have a healthy, shiny, clean, and mat-free coat.

• When housebreaking a puppy, wait until spring to train it to the outdoors. Puppies are susceptible to the cold and are hard to train in the winter. Paper-train him inside instead.

• Cats who go outside sometimes like to stay warm on or under the hood of car. Before someone in your family starts the car, be sure to bang on the hood and sides, and check to see that the cat is clear of it. Cats may also perch on top of a wheel, out of sight, and could be seriously injured when the car starts up.

• Even tiny doses of antifreeze are poisonous for dogs and cats. Animals are attracted to its sweet taste. Be sure you or the adults in your household clean up spills thoroughly.

Hot Weather Tips

• Never leave your pet in a car, which can quickly turn into an oven, even with the windows slightly open and the car parked in the shade. Open windows do not provide enough ventilation, and the shade shifts with the sun as the day moves along. Also, if the car windows are open too widely, your pet may jump out of the car and get lost.

• Always give your pet plenty of cool, clean water. When traveling, carry a thermos filled with cool water for your pet.

• Never force your dog to exercise after he or she eats, especially in very hot, humid weather. Instead, exercise your pet in the cool of the day—early morning and late afternoon or early evening.

• Provide plenty of shade for a dog that stays outside. A properly built doghouse is best. Bring your dog (or cat) inside during the hottest part of the day and let your pet rest in a cool part of the house.

• Never take your pet to the beach. This is not considerate of other beachgoers since dogs sometimes relieve themselves on the beach. Also, a romp in the surf or a dig in the wet sand is little comfort when there is no shade to lie in and no fresh water to drink.

• Keep your pet well groomed. Don't shave off its coat, because it gives your pet protection against heat and insects. A clean, groomed coat will help protect your pet against summer skin problems.

• Never go on vacation and leave your pet shut in an empty house or tied up outside. Be sure to get someone to feed and care for it while you're gone.

• If you and your family are renting a house for all or part of the summer, never, *ever* adopt a pet "just for the vacation time." Too many pets are abandoned this way and end up injured, dead, or destroyed in animal shelters.

• Watch out for fleas and ticks (especially deer ticks that cause Lyme Disease) that may infect your pet. Take your cat or dog to the vet for a summer checkup, and use a good flea and tick repellent recommended by your vet. It's a good idea to check your pet for ticks every so often.

• Never walk or let your pet outside in areas that have been sprayed with insecticides or other chemicals. Pets can easily become poisoned by sprays for weeds, insects, and pests. Keep your pet away from these areas and watch him or her carefully for signs of illness.

Eight Travel Tips

1. Always take your pet's own food and water bowls. You might want to bring the semi-moist packaged type of food. It's easier to handle and open. Bring a thermos or canteen of fresh water and offer some to your pet when you're about to have a cool drink.

2. Pets should never be given tranquilizers on a trip without your vet's approval.

3. Always secure your pet with a leash when you open your car window, and never open windows all the way. Cats and dogs may jump out of the car. In hot weather, use the car's cooling ventilation system or air conditioning to cool off the car whenever possible.

4. As mentioned before, never leave your pet alone in the car in hot or cold weather. Another reason not to do this is that your pet may be stolen by animal thieves, who make money by stealing pets and selling them illegally to research laboratories and kennels.

5. Always keep your pet in the car with you and not inside a camper or trailer, or in the back of a pickup truck. Pets in pickup trucks sometimes jump out. And by keeping your pet with you, you can tell when he or she is hungry, thirsty, hot, or tired.

6. Remember that when you're ready to make a bathroom stop, your pet is probably ready to go, too.

7. Try to leave plenty of time—six hours or more—between a pet feeding and your departure, if your pet is not used to car trips. He or she may get car sick.

8. Bring along your cat's litter pan with litter in it. You or an adult can easily carry it inside a plastic garbage bag.

First Aid for Pets

It's a good idea to know basic first aid for sick or injured pets in case you can't reach your vet right away, or when seconds count. Ask your vet about medicines such as stimulants and sedatives that can be kept in the house in case your pet needs them. These medicines should be given to your pet by an adult acting on the vet's instructions.

Internal Bleeding

Head injuries, fractures, falls, diseases, and infections can cause internal bleeding. Symptoms are fainting, paleness, weak pulse, shallow breathing, bleeding from nose, mouth, or other parts of the body. Keep your pet quiet and well covered with the head lower than the hind quarters.

External Bleeding

Apply pressure directly on the wound, using a clean cloth soaked in cold water. Maintain a steady pressure until clot is formed. Give your pet warm water to drink but never a stimulant.

Shock

Shock is caused by fright, loss of blood, severe injuries, or exposure to extreme heat or cold. Symptoms are unconsciousness, semi-consciousness, cold body, jerky breathing, bluish-white gums, or involuntary urination. Keep your pet warm. Revive an unconscious animal with a pad saturated with ammonia under its nose. Artificial respiration is indicated if breathing has stopped. Never give a sedative.

Poisoning

Too many pets are poisoned when insecticides, roach powders, shoe dyes, hair dyes, lye, and cleaning fluids are left where animals can reach them.

Seconds count when getting as much poison out of your pet's system as possible. Induce vomiting with Epsom salts in warm water (one teaspoonful to a glass of warm water), or 3-percent-strength hydrogen peroxide mixed with equal parts of water. Peroxide will act as an antidote for phosphorus, frequently used in rat poisons, and Epsom salts help combat lead and arsenic poisoning. Egg white beaten into milk should be given if your pet has taken one of the mercuric compounds. For food poisoning, give an enema, followed by Epsom salts. A solution of table salt combats thallium, found in bug poisons. Vinegar is the antidote for alkali. Read labels on all household or garden products to see what they are made of.

Broken Bones

Apply a temporary splint made of board, padded with a soft cloth. Rush your pet to a veterinarian. Handle all fractures as little as possible, since movement may cause sharp bone ends to cut blood vessels or nerves.

Burns

Cut away burned hair and apply petroleum jelly, a thin paste of sodium bicarbonate, or cold-tea compresses. Cover lightly with gauze.

Heat Exhaustion

Too much heat can cause your pet to become listless, semi-conscious, or unconscious; the skin cold, the eyes blurred; with possible muscle cramps. Keep your pet in a cool room and immediately give it water containing small amounts of table salt. Do not give bicarbonate of soda.

Heat Stroke

This is caused by too much heat, direct hot sun, high humidity, and lack of air. Symptoms differ from heat exhaustion in that the skin becomes dry and hot. The animal is weak and does not move. Muscle cramps and twitching may accompany a fever up to 110°F. Shock, circulatory collapse, and even death may follow. Immediately place your pet in a tub containing cold water, or shower him or her with cold water, and massage skin thoroughly.

Health Insurance for Pets

Many people have health insurance that helps them to pay doctor and hospital bills in case they get sick. Now this kind of insurance is available for dogs and cats in every American state except Tennessee. The insurance usually covers major injuries and accidents. To find out more about animal insurance companies in your state, contact your vet, an animal shelter, or the A.S.P.C.A.

What to Do if Your Pet Gets Lost

Do's

• Stay calm and think positively. You won't help your pet if you panic.

• Write a description of your pet, including sex, breed, color, age, height, scars, stitches, and any other identifying information. Give copies to your local newspaper, animal shelters, and humane societies.

• Visit animal shelters near where your pet was last seen. Tell shelter workers you are looking for your pet, so that they'll be on the lookout, too. Give them your phone number. Let the workers at these shelters get to know you and your pet.

• Make a poster that looks like this:

• Use phone numbers only, no names (except for those of animal shelters) on your poster.

• The reward doesn't have to be huge, but you may want to offer something to the person who finds your pet. You and your family should decide how much of a reward seems fair.

• Put up a lot of posters around your town or city, about every six blocks from where your pet was last seen. Make sure that they are at the eye level of an average-sized adult or older child. Place posters at corners, so that they can be seen from all directions. Check posters every two to three days to make sure they are still in good, readable condition.

• Send posters to humane societies and animal shelters.

• Follow up *all* leads immediately, and always take an adult with you when you meet a person who claims to have found your pet.

• Check the lost-and-found sections of as many newspapers as possible every day.

Don'ts

• Don't run around looking for your pet unless you are positive you know where he or she is.

• Don't expect your pet to come home on its own, especially after 48 hours have passed.

• Don't include your pet's name on your poster, or in the description given to newspapers. If your pet was stolen, the thief will have greater control over your pet if he or she knows its name.

• Don't tell a stranger the value of your purebred. You might end up paying ransom to an animal thief.

PETFINDERS

Petfinders is a nonprofit organization that will help you find your lost pet. When you call Petfinders, a description of your pet is entered in the organization's computer. The computer matches the description with those of animals that have been lost or found up to 60 miles from your home. Petfinders also sends out a Lost Pet Report with a Petfinders registration number to all animal shelters, humane societies, and rescue leagues within the 60-mile radius. The organization will also send you a publication titled "What to Do When You Lose Your Pet." Petfinders is located in New York City, but it carries out searches nationwide.

The cost of a one-time Petfinders search is $49. A lifetime membership costs $24.50 and includes a tag with Petfinders' toll-free number and the member's serial number; a computer entry with a description of the pet and the owner's phone number; and a signed authorization from the owner allowing Petfinders to contact a veterinarian or a kennel in case of an emergency. About one out of three lost pets has been found by Petfinders.

To contact Petfinders, call 1-800-666-LOST or 1-800-666-5678.

Animal Associations and Societies

Listed below are some associations and societies that are dedicated to the well-being of animals. You might want to write and ask them for information on their publications, newsletters, posters, calendars or events, or membership fees, if any.

- American Horse Protection Association
  1038 31st St. NW
  Washington, D.C. 20007

- American Horse Shows Association
  220 E. 42nd St.
  New York, NY 10017-5806

- American Kennel Club
  51 Madison Ave.
  New York, NY 10010

- American Society for the Prevention of Cruelty to Animals (ASPCA)
  441 E. 92nd St.
  New York, NY 10128

- Cat Fanciers Association
  1309 Allaire Ave.
  Ocean, NJ 07712

- Guide Dog Foundation for the Blind
  371 Jericho Tpke.
  Smithtown, NY 11787

- Humane Society of the U.S.
  2100 L St. NW
  Washington, D.C. 20037

- National Audubon Society
  950 Third Ave.
  New York, NY 10022

- National Horse Show Assocaition of America, LTD
  680 5th Ave. #1602
  New York, NY 10017-5806

- National Wildlife Federation
  1412 16th St. NW
  Washington, D.C. 20036

- World Wildlife Fund
  1255 23rd St. NW
  Washington, D.C. 20037

Index of Illustrations

Index